Lead with PACE

From Chaos to Clarity

How Leaders Execute and Sustain Lasting Transformation

Bhaviik Kumar

Lead with PACE
From Chaos to Clarity: How Leaders Execute and Sustain Lasting Transformation

First Edition: 2025

This is a work of non-fiction. Any references to individuals, companies, or events are drawn from the author's experience and are either used with permission or anonymized for educational purposes.

Printed in Bharat.

For rights inquiries, speaking engagements, or consulting opportunities, contact:
Email: connect@bhaviikkumar.com
Website: www. bhaviikkumar.com

ISBN: 978-93-344-2498-0

DEDICATION

To the Builders, Not Just the Dreamers

To every leader who dared to execute when it was easier to stay in strategy. To those who stayed grounded in purpose, even when the world chased perfection.

And most of all, to my mentors—who taught me that action, not ambition, defines a life well-lived.

ACKNOWLEDGMENTS

This book was not written alone.

I am deeply grateful to the many mentors, colleagues, clients, and changemakers who shaped my understanding of leadership—not through theory, but through lived experience.

To my team and collaborators who believed in the PACE model when it was just an idea on paper—thank you for your courage, feedback, and trust.

To the professionals who shared stories of transformation, failure, and reinvention—you gave this book its heartbeat.

A special thanks to my editors, readers, and sounding boards—you refined the rough stone into something worthy.

And finally, to my family. Your unwavering belief and quiet sacrifices made space for this book to be born. You are my daily PACE—my purpose, my accountability, my compass, and my fuel.

To my daughter—thank you for teaching me patience, wonder and the quiet strength of love.

CONTENTS

CHAPTER ONE

The Leadership Crisis

Why Transformation Fails Without Execution

"Vision is a headline. Execution is the story that makes it true."

Inspiration Without Execution Is Illusion

The room is electric. Slides shimmer with bold colours. The CEO's voice rises: *"We will redefine our industry, double our market share, and lead the future!"* Applause erupts, hashtags start trending, and headlines gush about the company's daring vision.

Fast-forward twelve months. The stock price is flat, frontline teams are confused, and projects lie half-built. Nobody remembers the applause; everybody feels the fatigue. What happened?

Leadership today suffers not from a shortage of vision but from a shortage of follow-through. Every year, boardrooms announce bold strategies – digital transformation, cultural reinvention, operational excellence – yet most never materialize beyond the PowerPoint slide. It's not that leaders don't dream big enough. It's that the bridge from idea to outcome collapses under its own weight.

Most executives overestimate the power of inspiration. They believe that if they set a compelling vision, the organization will find a way. But inspiration is only ignition – it sparks movement; it doesn't sustain it. Execution is the engine that carries vision to reality. Without it, strategy is little more than theatre.

The harsh truth: most organizations don't fail for lack of ambition. They fail because ambition never turns into action. That gap – between what leaders say and what teams actually do – is the silent killer of transformation.

The Shock Truth: Strategy Rarely Becomes Reality

Consider this: studies across industries consistently show that **70% of strategic initiatives fail to achieve their intended outcomes**. That means for every ten bold announcements, only three cross the finish line. The rest stall in meetings, lose momentum in bureaucracy, or fade into irrelevance as priorities shift.

Yet inside boardrooms, the story told is different. Leaders convince themselves the plan is working because dashboards glow green, decks are polished, and language sounds confident. But beneath the surface, teams are confused, coordination is weak, and progress is incremental at best.

The uncomfortable truth is that **inspiration is not the same as execution**. One happens on stage; the other happens in the trenches. And too many organizations stop at the stage.

The Execution Gap: Where Bold Ideas Go to Die

The space between vision and delivery – the **execution gap** – is where most transformations falter. It's not an abstract concept; it's painfully visible on the ground:

- Strategy launches with fanfare, then disappears into the noise of day-to-day operations.
- Teams receive goals but not guardrails, leading to scattered efforts and wasted energy.
- Leaders celebrate intent while ignoring the absence of outcomes.

The result is a credibility deficit: employees grow cynical, customers grow impatient, and stakeholders lose confidence.

A mid-sized enterprise learned this the hard way when a high-profile digital overhaul consumed two years and millions in investment – only to deliver a fraction of promised impact. Strategy documents were beautiful. All-hands meetings were inspiring. But accountability was vague, decision rights unclear, and feedback loops absent. What began as a bold bet ended as an expensive lesson: **vision without execution is delusion.**

The Three S's of Execution Failure

Across industries, three silent forces widen the execution gap. They operate quietly, often unnoticed, but together they derail even the best strategies.

1. **Scatter:** Efforts spread across too many priorities. Everyone is busy; nothing moves.
2. **Silence:** Difficult truths about progress are hidden, replaced with optimistic status updates.
3. **Stall:** Decision-making slows as accountability diffuses and ownership blurs.

These forces are rarely intentional. They creep in when planning stops at aspiration. Leaders announce a vision and assume alignment will follow. It rarely does.

The Bridge Test: A Leadership Gut Check

Here's a simple test for any leader: pick your boldest initiative and walk it down the hall. Can every team explain:

- What this initiative means for them?
- What they are accountable for?
- What progress looks like this week?

If not, your bridge between vision and execution is incomplete. Most leaders fail this test – not because they lack intelligence or will, but because they mistake clarity at the top for clarity everywhere. It isn't.

What Execution-Centric Leadership Looks Like

Execution-centric leadership looks and feels different. It shifts focus from *what we want to become* to *how we will get there* – and it shows up in daily practices, not just annual plans.

It starts with ruthless prioritization: narrowing ambition to a few critical bets rather than many scattered efforts. It demands visible ownership: every milestone must have a name, not a committee. And it relies on fast feedback: learning loops that surface problems early and adjust course quickly.

One manufacturing organization reversed a failing turnaround by applying these principles. Instead of launching ten simultaneous workstreams, leadership focused on three. Each had a single accountable owner, clear success metrics, and weekly progress loops. Within a year, cost overruns dropped by 30% and customer satisfaction improved. The bold vision didn't change – but execution finally caught up.

Execution Is a Culture, Not a Checklist

The biggest misconception is that execution is about tools – dashboards, trackers, KPIs. These matter, but they're secondary. Execution is fundamentally about **culture**: a shared belief that what we say will happen *must* happen, and that everyone is responsible for making it so.

In high-execution cultures:

- **Language shifts** from "we should" to "we will."
- **Meetings end** with commitments, not just conversations.
- **Success is measured** not by effort or activity but by outcomes delivered.

Leaders set this tone. When they treat commitments casually, teams follow. When they hold themselves accountable publicly – admitting missteps, resetting course, and modelling ownership – accountability cascades through the organization.

The Human Cost of the Execution Gap

The execution gap isn't just a business problem; it's a human one. When promises aren't fulfilled, trust erodes. Teams grow disengaged. Cynicism replaces commitment. People stop believing that leadership means what it says.

And once trust is gone, no strategy – no matter how brilliant – can succeed.

Bridging the Gap Requires a New Leadership Framework

The leaders who consistently deliver don't simply inspire; they **translate vision into motion**. They treat strategy not as an event but as a living system – one that is planned, owned, communicated, and reinforced daily.

This is where the **PACE Framework** begins its work. Built from the ground up to close the execution gap, PACE is not another leadership theory. It is a practical operating system for turning bold intentions into measurable outcomes.

But before we explore how it works, we must first dismantle the illusions that prevent execution from taking root. And that begins with the myths leaders tell themselves about accountability and ownership – myths that keep organizations stuck in the gap.

The Three Myths That Keep Leaders Stuck

If the execution gap is so well-documented, why do even the most capable leaders fall into it again and again? The answer lies in the **stories leaders tell themselves** – comforting myths that explain away failure, justify inertia, and disguise systemic problems as isolated incidents. These myths feel intuitive. They're repeated so often they sound like truth. Yet they quietly undermine accountability, diffuse ownership, and keep organizations spinning their wheels.

To bridge the execution gap, leaders must first confront and dismantle these myths.

Myth 1: The Hero Leader Will Save Us

Modern business culture glorifies the "hero leader" – the charismatic visionary who rallies teams with speeches, sets audacious goals, and single-handedly steers the ship through storms. Boards hire them. Media celebrates them. Teams wait for them. And in doing so, organizations unconsciously outsource accountability upward.

The belief that one extraordinary leader can solve systemic execution challenges is seductive – and dangerous. Because when results don't follow, the explanation becomes: *"We need a stronger leader."* The real problem – lack of systems, shared ownership, and execution discipline – remains untouched.

An organization learned this the hard way during a multi-year transformation. A new CEO arrived with a sterling reputation, bold vision, and sweeping promises.

Employees initially rallied behind the leader's charisma. But beneath the surface, decision rights remained unclear, frontline managers lacked empowerment, and execution routines were absent. The CEO worked harder, spoke louder, and pushed harder – but the system didn't change. Two years later, the company was still struggling with the same issues. The myth of the hero leader had masked the real work needed.

True leadership is not about being the saviour. It's about being the architect of systems where execution happens reliably – with or without the leader in the room. Hero leaders might inspire teams to start; systems and shared accountability are what sustain results.

Leadership shift: From "I will save this" to "We will build this."

Myth 2: Empowerment Alone Drives Accountability

The second myth is subtler – and more pervasive. Many organizations, burned by command-and-control cultures, swing to the opposite extreme: "Just empower people." They assume that if authority is pushed downward and autonomy is granted, accountability will naturally follow.

But empowerment without clarity is abdication, not leadership. Autonomy is powerful **only** when people know what they are accountable for, how success is defined, and what support systems exist.

A mid-sized enterprise learned this when it reorganized into self-managed teams. Leaders proudly declared, "You have full ownership." But they failed to clarify decision rights, align metrics, or define boundaries. Teams made conflicting decisions, duplicated efforts, and worked at cross-purposes. Instead of unleashing ownership, empowerment became chaos. Morale dropped, and performance slipped.

Empowerment is a powerful ingredient – but it is not the meal. Accountability still requires **clear outcomes, defined roles**, and **visible feedback**. Without them, "empowerment" is an empty slogan.

Imagine telling a rowing team, "You're all empowered – row however you like." One row left, another right, a third stops to adjust the oar. The boat spins in circles. Empowerment without direction is motion without progress.

Leadership shift: From "Empowerment is enough" to "Empowerment must be anchored in clarity."

Myth 3: Agile Solves Execution

The third myth is a modern one: the belief that adopting Agile – or any popular methodology – will magically fix execution. Leaders assume that if they install the right framework, accountability will follow. But process alone doesn't change culture. And Agile without ownership is just speed without direction.

A technology company discovered this during a product overhaul. Inspired by startup success stories, they rolled out Agile across hundreds of teams. Ceremonies multiplied: stand-ups, retrospectives, sprints. Boards filled with sticky notes. But despite the new vocabulary, velocity barely improved. Projects still missed deadlines. Dependencies remained unmanaged. Ownership was diffuse.

Agile had optimized activity, not outcomes. Teams sprinted – but not always in the right direction. Without clear priorities, decision rights, and accountability for results, Agile became theatre.

Agile is powerful when it rests on an accountability foundation. It demands clarity on the "why" before iteration on the "how." Without that, it risks accelerating confusion.

Installing Agile without accountability is like upgrading a car's engine without fixing the steering. You go faster – but not necessarily where you need to go.

Leadership shift: From "Agile drives execution" to "Accountability powers Agile."

The Cost of These Myths

These myths aren't just intellectual errors – they carry real-world costs:

- **Energy drain:** Teams work hard but pull in different directions.
- **Strategic drift:** Priorities shift constantly because no one owns outcomes.
- **Cultural erosion:** Cynicism takes root when big promises yield small results.

Over time, the organization stops believing in change at all. "We've seen this before," employees mutter. "It won't stick." And that cynicism becomes the greatest obstacle of all.

A leading financial services company once spent millions on a digital transformation that stalled repeatedly. Every post-mortem blamed different things – leadership turnover, lack of empowerment, methodology issues. But the root cause was always the same: accountability lived nowhere. No single leader owned cross-functional outcomes. Teams optimized for their silos. Systems tracked activity, not commitments. By the time leadership confronted this truth, competitors had pulled far ahead.

When accountability is missing, even the best strategy becomes theatre. These myths provide comforting excuses for why execution fails. But excuses do not close the gap – ownership does.

What Execution-Ready Leadership Looks Like

Leaders who consistently deliver results reject these myths and embrace a different mindset – one built on **distributed accountability, systemic clarity, and cultural ownership.**

Here's what that looks like:

- They **reject the hero narrative.** Leadership is measured not by how much they do themselves, but by how effectively they build systems where others deliver.
- They **design empowerment deliberately.** Autonomy is earned, structured, and supported – not dumped and forgotten.
- They **treat methodologies as tools, not magic.** Agile, Lean, Six Sigma – all work only when powered by clear accountability.

Execution-ready leaders act less like generals issuing orders and more like gardeners cultivating growth. They create conditions – clarity, ownership, feedback – in which teams thrive. They understand that execution is not a moment of inspiration but a habit built over time.

From Myth to Mastery

The bridge from strategy to execution is built not on speeches, slogans, or frameworks but on **accountability deliberately designed into the fabric of leadership.** When leaders stop outsourcing execution to heroes, stop mistaking autonomy for ownership, and stop believing process can replace commitment, they unlock a new level of performance.

They build cultures where:

- Accountability is shared but never diffused.
- Empowerment is structured, not chaotic.
- Methodologies serve clarity, not substitute for it.

And most importantly, they shift the organizational story from *"We tried, but..."* to *"We promised, and we delivered."*

Beyond Myths Lies the Bill

Dispelling myths is only the beginning. As long as leaders remain trapped by them, execution failure is predictable. But the consequences go deeper than missed KPIs or delayed projects. The real cost is paid in **trust, culture, and credibility** – the invisible balance sheet of leadership.

And that's where we turn next: the hidden bill organizations pay when accountability fails.

The Bill We Pay for the Execution Gap

When accountability falters and execution stalls, the consequences extend far beyond missed KPIs or delayed projects. The most dangerous costs are often invisible – eroding trust, corroding culture, and draining credibility. These losses don't show up on quarterly reports, but they shape everything that follows. They determine whether future strategies inspire commitment or roll eyes, whether teams rise to challenges or retreat into cynicism.

Let's examine the three invisible costs leaders pay when execution fails.

1. Trust: The First Casualty

Trust is the currency of leadership. It is built when promises are kept – and it evaporates when they aren't. Every time a bold initiative is launched with fanfare and dies quietly in execution, leaders spend that currency. Over time, teams stop believing not only in the project but in the people leading it.

An enterprise launched three consecutive transformation programs over five years. All three began with optimism and investment. All three fizzled – mired in cross-functional misalignment, shifting priorities, and poor follow-through. By the fourth attempt, something had changed: attendance at kick-off meetings dropped, engagement surveys fell, and employees described new initiatives as "just another flavour of the month."

Nothing about the fourth program was inherently weaker than the first. But trust – the soil in which execution grows – had been depleted.

Trust, once broken, is difficult to rebuild. It is not restored by new slogans or more ambitious goals. It is rebuilt through delivery – one kept promise at a time. Until then, even the best strategies are received with scepticism.

Leadership lesson: Every unkept commitment writes an IOU against future credibility.

2. Culture: From Ownership to Cynicism

The second cost is cultural – the erosion of ownership. Cultures are shaped less by what leaders say than by what they *repeat*. When organizations repeatedly launch initiatives that don't deliver, people adapt. They become more cautious. They stop raising ideas. They disengage from strategy conversations because they no longer believe their energy will matter.

One senior leader described this cultural slide as "organizational learned helplessness." Over time, people stop expecting things to change, even when they want them to. They start showing up for meetings physically but checking out mentally. Execution becomes "someone else's job."

At a manufacturing company, a poorly executed restructuring left teams with shifting roles and unclear priorities. Months later, even unrelated projects struggled. Employees hesitated to make decisions without sign-off. Managers waited for instructions before acting. A culture that had once been agile became risk-averse and slow.

Cynicism is not just a mood – it's a strategy-killer. Once it takes root, even good ideas fail because people no longer invest belief or discretionary effort. Reversing that trajectory requires more than motivational speeches. It requires leaders to demonstrate, through consistent action, that what they say will happen *does* happen.

Leadership lesson: Culture follows credibility. When execution breaks, culture bends – and not in your favour.

3. Credibility: The Long-Term Debt

The third cost is credibility – the invisible balance sheet on which future strategies depend. Every unfulfilled initiative chips away at leadership's authority. Stakeholders begin to doubt forecasts. Investors question guidance. Customers hesitate to trust promises. Even small failures accumulate into a reputation for overpromising and underdelivering.

A fast-growing fintech once promised a revolutionary new platform within 18 months. Delays mounted. Milestones were missed. Deadlines shifted silently. By the time the platform launched – over two years late – customers had lost faith, competitors had captured market share, and internal morale had collapsed. The technology eventually caught up, but the company's reputation never fully did.

Credibility is hard-won and easily lost. And once lost, it infects every future initiative. Teams resist new projects not because they lack belief in the idea but because they no longer believe in leadership's ability to deliver it.

Leadership lesson: Without credibility, even the best ideas cannot gain traction.

The Hidden Spiral

These three costs – trust, culture, credibility – don't operate in isolation. They reinforce one another in a downward spiral:

1. Execution failure breaks **trust**.
2. Eroded trust undermines **culture**, replacing ownership with cynicism.
3. A weakened culture damages **credibility**, reducing belief in future efforts.
4. Damaged credibility makes future execution even harder.

The spiral accelerates until leaders intervene. And the longer it runs, the harder it is to reverse. At some point, teams stop failing *at* execution and start failing *before* execution – because they never truly commit.

Introducing PACE: Closing the Gap from Vision to Reality

The good news: the spiral is not inevitable. It can be reversed – and prevented – when leaders move beyond inspiration to build a system that reliably turns intent into outcomes. That system is the **PACE Framework**: a leadership operating system designed to close the execution gap by hardwiring accountability into how organizations plan, act, communicate, and engage.

PACE is not another buzzword. It is the distilled result of years of transformation work across industries – from manufacturing floors to boardrooms, from digital overhauls to cultural turnarounds. It is built for one purpose: to help leaders deliver what they promise.

The PACE Framework at a Glance

PACE stands for **Planning, Accountability, Communication, and Engagement** – four interconnected pillars that form the backbone of execution. Each is powerful on its own; together, they create a self-reinforcing system that aligns ambition with action.

1. **Planning – Aligning Strategy with Reality**
   Planning is where execution begins. It's the discipline of translating vision into actionable roadmaps – ones that sequence priorities, anticipate risks, and create shared clarity. Planning breaks big ambitions into measurable milestones and names the owners who will deliver them. It shifts conversations from "what we want" to "how we'll do it."

Leadership question: Are we chasing ambition, or are we designing execution?

2. **Accountability – Turning Ownership into Outcomes**
   Accountability is the engine of execution. It's what converts commitments into delivery. In practice, this means clarifying decision rights, defining outcomes, and embedding feedback loops that surface gaps before they become failures. Accountability is not about blame – it's about building a culture where people own results as deeply as they own ideas.

Leadership question: Is every priority attached to a single name – and do they know it?

3. **Communication – Building Ecosystems of Understanding**
   Execution collapses when messages don't land. Communication in PACE is not about broadcasting information but creating shared understanding that drives coordinated action. It's about turning complexity into clarity, purpose into narrative, and instructions into commitment. Done well, it aligns thousands of micro-decisions to the same North Star.

Leadership question: Does everyone understand not just what we're doing, but why it matters and how their work contributes?

4. **Engagement – Sustaining Momentum Through People**
   Execution is not a one-time event – it's a sustained effort. Engagement fuels that effort. It's how leaders turn compliance into commitment and teams into co-owners of outcomes. Engagement is about listening as much as leading, shaping culture as much as process, and creating an environment where people *want* to deliver, not just *have* to.

Leadership question: Are our people energized by the mission, or merely executing tasks?

Why PACE Works: The System, Not the Silo

Most organizations treat these four elements as separate functions – planning as a strategy exercise, accountability as a performance system, communication as a messaging task, and engagement as HR's job. That siloed approach is why execution breaks down. PACE works because it integrates them into a single, reinforcing loop:

- **Planning** gives direction.
- **Accountability** ensures follow-through.
- **Communication** aligns action.
- **Engagement** sustains energy.

Together, they create a rhythm where strategy moves forward predictably – not in bursts of heroics but in a steady drumbeat of delivery.

An enterprise that had failed three previous transformation attempts finally succeeded when it embraced this system. Instead of launching yet another strategy deck, leaders began with a planning reset: one shared roadmap, clear milestones, and named owners. They overhauled accountability rituals, introduced transparent communication practices, and rebuilt engagement from the ground up. Within 18 months, on-time project delivery jumped from 42% to 86%, and employee confidence in leadership rose by double digits.

The vision hadn't changed – but the system behind it had.

From Program to Practice

PACE is not a project you launch once. It is a way of leading. It embeds accountability into everyday rhythms:

- Quarterly reviews become **learning loops** rather than blame sessions.
- Strategy offsites end with **clear ownership**, not just inspiration.
- Meetings conclude with **commitments**, not just conversations.
- Engagement isn't an annual survey – it's a daily dialogue.

Leaders who adopt PACE stop relying on bursts of energy and start building structures that sustain execution. They move from **announcing change** to **delivering change**.

Turning Intent into Impact

Here's how PACE played out in practice. Arjun, a seasoned COO hired to rescue a global supply chain initiative that had stalled twice before. The strategy was strong, but execution lagged: departments worked in silos, accountability was diffuse, and communication resembled a maze.

Arjun's first move wasn't to rewrite the strategy. It was to apply PACE.

- **Planning:** He scrapped sprawling slide decks and created a one-page roadmap with five mission-critical priorities, each linked to specific outcomes.
- **Accountability:** He named single owners for each milestone and instituted weekly review loops focused on learning, not blame.
- **Communication:** He simplified messaging into plain language, connecting every deliverable to the larger mission.
- **Engagement:** He involved frontline managers in redesigning workflows, turning sceptics into co-owners.

Within six months, cross-functional misalignment plummeted, decision-making accelerated, and delivery pace doubled. The same people, the same strategy – but now powered by a system designed for execution.

Arjun's success wasn't magic. It was method. PACE turned scattered effort into coordinated movement. It transformed a plan on paper into outcomes in reality.

Stop Announcing. Start Building.

The leadership crisis of our time is not a crisis of vision. It's a crisis of execution. And solving it doesn't require louder speeches, new slogans, or trendier frameworks. It requires a system designed for delivery – one that hardwires accountability into the daily life of the organization.

The PACE Framework is that system. It is the bridge between the world leaders imagine and the one they build. It transforms leadership from a performance into a practice, from an event into a habit, from inspiration into impact.

The execution gap is not inevitable. It is a choice. And leaders who choose to close it redefine what's possible – for their organizations, their people, and themselves.

From Intent to Impact: Arjun's Story

To understand what execution-focused leadership looks like in practice, let's step into the story of **Arjun**, a seasoned operations leader who inherited a transformation initiative already written off as a failure.

A Plan Without Progress

When Arjun joined a manufacturing company as COO, the organization was two years into an ambitious transformation to modernize its supply chain. The vision was strong – digitize operations, reduce lead times, and create an agile, customer-centric network. The problem was that almost nothing was working.

Three rounds of restructuring had produced reams of new org charts but little change on the ground. Departments worked in silos, each chasing its own priorities. Accountability was vague – no one could say who owned which milestones. Communication was heavy on reports but light on clarity. And morale was sinking as teams endured yet another "transformation" that seemed destined to fail.

Arjun didn't question the vision. But he immediately saw the real problem: **this was not an execution failure – it was an execution vacuum.** The company had ambition but no operating system to translate that ambition into results.

Step 1: Rewriting the Code

Arjun's first move wasn't another rallying speech. It was a reset.

He gathered his leadership team and asked a deceptively simple question:
"What are the five outcomes we must deliver in the next 12 months – and who owns each one?"

The room fell silent. PowerPoints were plentiful, but clear ownership was not. Arjun pressed until every outcome had a single accountable owner. And with that, he introduced the first pillar of **PACE – Planning**. The sprawling initiative was distilled into a focused roadmap of five priorities, each broken into milestones and mapped against timelines and dependencies.

Gone were vague aspirations like "enhance supply chain visibility." In their place: "Reduce average lead time from 26 to 18 days by Q4." Each outcome was measurable. Each milestone had a name attached.

Planning was no longer a document. It was a discipline.

Step 2: Making Accountability Real

Next came the second pillar – **Accountability**.

Arjun introduced a weekly "Accountability Cadence" – short, structured reviews focused on commitments and outcomes. Meetings shifted from status updates ("We're working on it") to accountability conversations ("We committed to reducing backlog by 12%. We achieved 8%. Here's why. Here's the fix.").

Accountability also meant changing language. Instead of asking, "What happened?" Arjun asked, "What did we learn?" Mistakes weren't punished; they were mined for lessons. Ownership became something people claimed, not something imposed.

A subtle cultural shift followed. Teams that once deflected responsibility began stepping forward. Managers who once hid behind reports began volunteering solutions. And the tone of leadership conversations changed – from excuses to execution.

Step 3: Communication as a Force Multiplier

Arjun knew that execution doesn't fail only because of poor planning or weak ownership. It also fails because of unclear communication. Strategies get lost in translation as they move through the layers of the organization. What starts as a bold idea at the top often reaches the frontline as a confusing memo.

To tackle this, Arjun simplified the message. He banned jargon in transformation updates and insisted that every leader explain initiatives in plain language a shop-floor employee could understand. He replaced lengthy slide decks with short narrative briefs answering four questions: **Why this matters, what success looks like, how we'll measure it, and who owns it.**

He also built feedback loops into communication. Monthly "pulse forums" brought frontline workers, middle managers, and executives into the same room to surface roadblocks and share progress stories. These sessions replaced polished presentations with real conversations – where insights flowed upward and decisions flowed downward.

The result was alignment. Everyone – from procurement analysts to plant supervisors – could articulate not just the goals but their role in achieving them. Communication stopped being noise and became a tool for coordinated action.

Step 4: Turning Engagement Into Ownership

The final piece was **Engagement** – perhaps the hardest and most overlooked pillar. Too often, organizations treat engagement as a survey or HR program. Arjun treated it as a leadership responsibility.

He began by involving people in problem-solving rather than announcing solutions from the top. When supply chain delays were traced to a packaging bottleneck, Arjun didn't convene a steering committee. He convened the packaging team. "How would you fix this if you owned the outcome?" he asked. Their recommendations shaped the solution – and because it was theirs, they owned its success.

He also shifted recognition away from individual heroics toward team accountability. Wins were celebrated not for who worked the longest hours but for who delivered outcomes. A new internal campaign highlighted "ownership stories" – moments when individuals stepped up and changed results. These stories spread faster than any memo and became part of the company's language.

Slowly, engagement transformed from compliance ("We're following orders") into commitment ("We're building this"). Execution energy, once top-down, became shared.

The Results: Momentum Becomes Movement

Within 12 months, the transformation that had stalled for two years was back on track. Lead times dropped by 30%. On-time delivery climbed by 25%. Operational costs fell. And employee engagement scores rose for the first time in five years.

More important than any metric was the shift in belief. People no longer rolled their eyes when new initiatives were announced. They leaned in. They trusted that promises would become reality – because they had lived through it.

Arjun's legacy wasn't just a successful transformation. It was a new operating rhythm for the company – one where bold vision met disciplined execution.

From Event to Operating System

Arjun's story reveals a crucial truth: execution excellence isn't built on individual brilliance or one-time interventions. It's built on systems that **make accountability inevitable and execution repeatable.**

Most organizations treat execution as a project – something that happens during "transformation phases" or "strategic initiatives." PACE turns it into an **operating system** – a way of thinking, deciding, communicating, and behaving that becomes part of daily life.

It's not about adding new tasks. It's about changing how the existing work is done.

- Planning shifts from annual exercises to continuous alignment.
- Accountability shifts from blame and compliance to ownership and delivery.
- Communication shifts from broadcasting to building shared understanding.
- Engagement shifts from participation to co-creation.

PACE makes execution not the responsibility of a few but the rhythm of the many.

Stop Announcing. Start Building.

Most leadership teams today do not suffer from a lack of ambition. They suffer from an addiction to *announcements.* New strategies. New values. New transformations. All launched with fanfare, all destined for the same graveyard if nothing changes.

The problem is not the vision. It's that vision remains trapped in the realm of intention. Leaders believe that clarity of purpose is enough, that once the "why" is shared, the "how" will follow. But in reality, purpose without process is potential without power.

And that is the leadership crisis of our time.

Execution is not glamorous. It is not a standing ovation after a town hall or a viral headline in the press. Execution is the quiet, relentless discipline of turning words into work and work into results. It's meetings that end with commitments. Reviews that end with learning. Plans that end with delivery.

It's leaders who stop mistaking motion for progress and start asking harder questions:

- Who owns this?
- What exactly will we deliver – and by when?
- What will we do differently when we fall short?
- How will we know, quickly, if we're off course?

And most importantly: **How will we build a system that makes execution the norm, not the exception?**

A New Leadership Contract

The world does not need more visionary statements. It needs leaders willing to sign a new contract with their organizations – one where *execution is not delegated, it is designed*. Where accountability is not demanded, it is modelled. Where communication is not performance, it is clarity. And where engagement is not a checkbox, it is the spark that turns teams into movements.

The future belongs to leaders who understand that execution is not the *end* of leadership – it is the essence of it.

It belongs to leaders who build bridges between intention and impact – and then walk across them with their teams.

It belongs to those who understand that **PACE is not a framework for projects. It is a discipline for leadership.**

Pause and Reflect

As you close this chapter, look at where vision outpaces execution in your organization and ask yourself:

- Where in your organization does vision soar but execution stumble – and why?
- How often do bold announcements fade into silence before they become results?
- Which comforting myths – like the hero leader or empowerment without clarity – might be holding your teams back?
- Are you measuring leadership by speeches given or by promises kept?
- What would change if you built your credibility not on ideas launched, but on outcomes delivered?

Next Step on the Journey

Leadership, at its core, is not about painting distant horizons – it's about building the road that leads there. Vision is the spark, but execution is the fire that warms the room. And when the bridge between intent and impact collapses, trust, culture, and credibility go with it.

Think of leadership like a great novel: vision is the opening line that hooks attention, but execution is the unfolding story that makes it true. As you step forward, remember – applause fades, but outcomes echo. The chapters ahead will show you how to close the gap between imagination and impact. And that begins with the quiet but transformative discipline that builds the bridge from dream to delivery: planning.

CHAPTER TWO

Planning

Building the Invisible Bridge Between Vision and Execution

"Planning is the courage to turn vision into steps, knowing the map will change but the compass must not."

The Planning Bridge

Leaders love vision. They craft bold declarations, deliver stirring speeches, and paint pictures of future success. But vision alone does not move an organization forward. Between ambition and achievement lies a wide gulf – the **Execution Gap** – and the only reliable bridge across it is **planning**.

Planning is often misunderstood as bureaucracy or delay. In reality, it is the discipline that turns intent into momentum – where ideas meet logistics and strategy meets action. Without planning, vision drifts into aspiration. With it, vision becomes a roadmap others can follow.

A Tale of Two Leaders

This is a story of two leaders working toward the same goal.

Arjun, the first, is a visionary. He announces an ambitious target and assumes execution will follow. Weeks later, teams are busy but misaligned. Departments pursue conflicting priorities. Deadlines slip. Arjun is frustrated: "I told them what success looks like. Why aren't they delivering?"

Maya shares a similar vision – but treats planning as sacred. After setting the goal, she breaks it into milestones, clarifies ownership, and builds rituals to track progress. The work is not glamorous: it involves spreadsheets, debates, and trade-offs. But within weeks, her teams know the destination, the steps, and their roles. When obstacles arise, they adapt quickly. Momentum builds.

Both leaders had vision. Only one built the bridge.

The Data Doesn't Lie

Research backs this up. McKinsey reports that nearly **70% of large-scale transformations fail**, not because of bad ideas but because leaders underestimate the discipline of planning. Harvard Business Review found that executives spend less than **10% of their time** on planning – yet it is the strongest predictor of execution success.

Organizations that treat planning as optional treat execution as a gamble. Few win.

Why Leaders Resist Planning

If planning is so vital, why do leaders avoid it? The reasons are human:

- **It's not glamorous.** Vision earns applause; planning happens behind closed doors.
- **It exposes uncertainty.** Planning forces leaders to confront what they don't know – timelines, risks, constraints.
- **It demands trade-offs.** Good planning means saying no to distractions and delaying pet projects.
- **It feels slow.** Many fear planning delays action – though skipping it causes far more rework later.
- **It challenges authority.** Planning invites debate and dissent, which insecure leaders perceive as loss of control.

In truth, planning is uncomfortable because it is honest – and honesty is the foundation of execution.

Reframing Planning as Leadership in Action

To embrace planning, leaders must see it not as "operational work" but as the essence of leadership:

- **Planning is decision-making.** It forces prioritization, sequencing, and resource allocation.
- **Planning is alignment.** It ensures everyone rows in the same direction.
- **Planning is foresight.** It surfaces risks before they become crises.
- **Planning is adaptability.** Done well, it builds feedback loops that allow rapid course correction.

Leaders who dismiss planning as beneath them abdicate their most critical role: translating vision into steps others can walk.

The Startup That Ran Too Fast

A mid-sized logistics-tech startup raised significant funding and set an ambitious goal: expand into five new markets in a year. Excitement was high – but planning was dismissed as "slowing things down." Teams were told to "just execute."

Sales launched simultaneously, but supply chains lagged. Customer support buckled. Regional teams built separate processes, duplicating effort. Within a year, money was gone, customers were frustrated, and employees burned out. Expansion stalled.

A peer company took a slower, planning-led approach. It sequenced market launches based on readiness, strengthened logistics ahead of time, and built playbooks for local teams. Growth started slower but proved sustainable – and within three years, it overtook the competitor.
The difference wasn't ambition. It was planning.

The Bridge Across the Execution Gap

Think of planning as a **bridge with three pillars**:

1. **Clarity of Destination**
    - Define the North Star.
    - Decide how success will be measured.

    - Assign clear ownership.
2. **Design of the Pathway**
    - Sequence milestones and map dependencies.
    - Anticipate risks.
    - Allocate resources intelligently.
3. **Rituals of Alignment**
    - Review progress regularly.
    - Update plans as realities shift.
    - Share lessons across teams.

A bridge built on only one or two pillars will collapse. All three are essential for crossing the execution gap.

Practical Ways to Build the Bridge

1. **Name the Execution Gap.** In your next leadership meeting, ask: *What stands between our vision and delivery?* Naming the gap is the first step to closing it.
2. **Make Planning a Discipline.** Treat it as ongoing work, not a kickoff exercise. Hold quarterly planning sprints and monthly reviews.
3. **Elevate Planning Champions.** Appoint leaders known for rigorous planning and celebrate them as much as visionaries.
4. **Communicate the Why.** Explain to teams that planning is not delay – it's insurance against chaos.
5. **Prototype a Plan.** Choose one initiative and build a full roadmap with milestones, owners, and risks. Use it as a template for others.

The Bridge Builder

Imagine two towns separated by a river. One mayor speaks passionately of trade and prosperity. The other quietly assembles builders, designs a bridge, and oversees its construction. Years later, one town is still dreaming while the other is thriving.

Vision may inspire, but **bridges deliver.** Leaders who plan are bridge builders. They turn ideas into reality.

Planning is not bureaucracy; it is leadership in motion. It is the **bridge** that carries vision across the execution gap. Without it, teams scatter, strategies dissolve, and momentum fades. With it, organizations move with clarity, focus, and resilience.

The first truth of execution is simple: **planning is not optional.** It is a leader's greatest act of service – the invisible work that makes everything else possible. The rest of this chapter will explore how to build effective roadmaps, avoid common planning failures, balance agility with stability, and make planning a cultural habit. But it all begins here: with leaders choosing to be bridge builders, not just dreamers.

The Fallacy of the Visionary Leader

Modern leadership culture glorifies the "visionary" – the charismatic figure who can see the future before others and rally people around a bold idea. From startup founders to political icons, vision is hailed as the pinnacle of leadership. But this celebration hides a dangerous illusion: **vision alone does not deliver results.** When leaders stop at vision and fail to translate it into structured plans, they often sabotage the very future they dream of creating. The result is organizations overflowing with passion but starved of traction.

The Seduction and Limits of Vision

Vision is seductive because it feels powerful. Declaring a bold future elevates leaders as courageous and inspiring. Teams find purpose in a mission that transcends day-to-day work. Yet vision's power has limits:

- It is **directional, not operational** – it tells us *where* to go, not *how* to get there.
- It is **inspiring but vague** – left unstructured, teams interpret it differently.
- It is **static** – while markets shift, competitors react, and crises erupt.

Vision is like a compass: necessary for orientation, but useless without a map. Leaders who stop at vision leave their teams wandering in execution fog.

When Vision Wasn't Enough

A mid-sized tech startup raised massive funding on the back of its founder's bold promise to "revolutionize logistics with AI." Media buzzed, employees rallied, and investors poured in. Yet within two years, the company collapsed. Why?

- No sequencing – teams built features simultaneously with no prioritization.
- No resource alignment – sales sold promises operations couldn't deliver.
- No risk planning – regulatory challenges blindsided them.
- No accountability – passion was everywhere, ownership was nowhere.

Vision wasn't the problem. The missing bridge – structured planning – was.

The Passion Trap

Another version of this fallacy is the belief that passion alone drives results. An NGO mobilized thousands around eradicating rural illiteracy. Volunteers were deeply committed – but without planning for training, material distribution, or measurement, the movement lost steam. Three years later, literacy rates were unchanged. **Passion without structure is like steam without a piston: powerful but unfocused.**

The Three Gaps of Visionary-Only Leadership

When leaders rely on vision without planning, three predictable gaps emerge:

1. **The Translation Gap** - Teams understand *what* to pursue but not *how* to do it.
2. **The Alignment Gap** - Departments interpret the vision differently, creating silos.
3. **The Adaptation Gap** - Leaders cling to outdated strategies as conditions change.

These gaps widen the Execution Gap – the chasm between aspiration and results.

Scaling Too Fast

A regional quick commerce company set out to dominate the country's digital retail space. The CEO's bold vision energized teams, but execution faltered. Infrastructure lagged, payment systems varied wildly, and local regulations were ignored. Customers left, operations buckled, and competitors surged ahead. Vision launched the journey, but the absence of disciplined planning sank it.

Vision and Planning: Partners, Not Opposites

Vision and planning are not rivals – they are complements:

- **Vision without planning** is a dream without traction.
- **Planning without vision** is activity without purpose.
- **Vision with planning** is leadership in execution.

Leaders must reject the notion that charisma or passion can substitute for clarity and discipline.

Escaping the Vision Trap

Leaders can avoid this trap with five deliberate practices:

1. **Translate Vision into Milestones**
   After declaring a bold goal, define the next three tangible outcomes.
   Example: Instead of "revolutionize customer experience," commit to "launch digital self-service in 3 months."
2. **Assign Named Owners**
   Every milestone must have a single accountable person. "The team" cannot own outcomes.
3. **Build Roadmaps, Not Speeches**
   Use planning tools to break vision into initiatives and projects. **Clarity beats charisma** in execution.
4. **Design Feedback Loops**
   Regularly test whether execution aligns with vision. Without loops, passion drifts into chaos.
5. **Revisit Assumptions**
   Explicitly state and review key assumptions. If conditions change, adjust plans – not just rhetoric.

The Lighthouse and the Shipbuilders

A lighthouse shows sailors the destination. It inspires, guides, and keeps them focused on the horizon. But a lighthouse cannot build ships, organize crews, or chart routes. Visionary leaders are lighthouses; planners are shipbuilders. **Only together can they reach new shores.**

Vision Paired with Discipline

A healthcare leader announced a bold goal: digitize patient records across dozens of hospitals. Instead of stopping at the "why," she invested in the "how." Pilots launched in three hospitals before scaling. Owners were assigned for IT, training, and change management. Rolling review loops refined implementation. Within three years, adoption exceeded 80%, and patient care improved dramatically. Her vision succeeded because planning carried it forward.

Beyond Inspiration, Toward Traction

The myth of the visionary leader persists because vision *feels* like leadership. But speeches don't ship products. Passion doesn't build systems. **True leadership is imagining the future – and then engineering the bridge to reach it.**

Followers don't just want inspiration; they want traction. And traction begins when vision is translated into milestones, ownership, and rituals. The next section explores how planning powers execution – and how leaders can make it their greatest competitive advantage.

The Invisible Bridge – How Planning Powers Execution

Planning rarely makes headlines. You won't see a CEO go viral for walking through a milestone chart, nor will shareholder letters praise sequencing with the same fervor as bold visions. Yet beneath the noise of ambition and charisma, planning is the quiet force that holds everything together. It is the **invisible bridge** across the Execution Gap – unseen from afar but carrying every person, decision, and process from idea to impact.

Organizations seldom fail for lack of vision. They fail because the bridge is weak or missing. Planning turns scattered effort into aligned motion, converts risk into resilience, and transforms ambition into repeatable results.

Why Planning Feels Invisible

Leaders often underestimate planning because its effects are subtle. It prevents problems before they surface, so success feels effortless. It creates alignment that looks "boringly consistent," so its value goes unnoticed. It enables adaptation, yet the pivot gets the credit, not the scaffolding that made it possible. That's the paradox: when planning works, it hides itself – until failure exposes its absence.

FMCG Expansion Done Right

An FMCG company preparing entry into three new regions spent six months meticulously mapping supply chains, forecasting demand, training distributors, and building playbooks. Competitors mocked the "delay." But when they launched, customers experienced seamless availability while competitors stumbled amid logistics chaos. Three years later, the planning-driven company tripled its market share. They built not just a vision – but the bridge to deliver it.

How Planning Powers Execution

Planning is not a static document; it's the engine that translates strategy into action. It does so through three invisible but powerful forces: **alignment, de-risking, and structured learning.**

1. Alignment – Creating One Direction

Without planning, departments interpret the same vision in conflicting ways. Marketing pursues one priority, operations another, finance a third. Energy scatters. Planning breaks the vision into shared milestones, clarifies ownership, and maps dependencies.

A logistics firm once faced chronic delays because operations optimized for cost while sales chased speed. Planning sessions revealed the misalignment and reset priorities. The result: a 30% drop in delays and rising customer satisfaction. Planning synchronized the rowing crew.

2. De-Risking – Anticipating the Unknown

Vision alone ignores risk; planning surfaces it. It identifies critical assumptions, maps potential obstacles, and sequences actions to test high-risk areas first.

A pharmaceutical company planning a global rollout identified regulatory approval as a major risk. Instead of waiting, they engaged regulators early and piloted approvals in test markets. The risk surfaced sooner, was addressed faster, and the rollout stayed on track.

3. Structured Learning – Turning Mistakes into Progress

Unplanned organizations repeat mistakes; planned ones turn them into insights. Planning builds learning loops – pilot before scaling, review before the next cycle, and adjust assumptions systematically.

A SaaS startup used rolling quarterly plans to review results and pivot three times in three years – not from failure, but from intentional learning. Each pivot sharpened their product-market fit and fueled rapid growth.

Why Leaders Misunderstand Planning

If planning is so essential, why do leaders resist it?

- **They confuse it with bureaucracy.** Thick binders and rigid forecasts masquerade as planning. True planning is lean, adaptive, and actionable.
- **They overvalue certainty.** Leaders seek perfect predictions, forgetting that plans are hypotheses to be tested, not prophecies to be obeyed.
- **They undervalue prevention.** Crises earn applause; prevention earns silence. But silence is success.

Planning is scaffolding. You don't admire scaffolding – you notice the building. Yet without it, the building collapses before completion. Planning disappears when work begins, but it was indispensable all along.

Practical Steps to Harness the Invisible Bridge

Leaders can actively build this bridge by:

1. **Declaring Assumptions** – Make them explicit and review them often.
2. **Sequencing Milestones** – Stage efforts: pilot → scale → optimize.
3. **Clarifying Ownership Early** – Assign one name per milestone, not a committee.
4. **Designing Feedback Rituals** – Test assumptions regularly and treat red flags as inputs, not punishments.
5. **Communicating Planning as Protection** – Reinforce that planning accelerates execution by preventing chaos.

A tech firm entering a new market took a "slow" approach: building partnerships, hiring locally, and tailoring strategies. Competitors mocked the pace – until they failed. By launch, the patient planner quietly captured market share, proving that invisible bridges often carry the heaviest loads.

Planning is invisible when it works – but its absence is painfully visible when it doesn't. It is the silent bridge that prevents drift, chaos, and collapse. Leaders who master planning don't just inspire; **they deliver.**

The next section explores **strategic roadmaps** – the tools that turn this invisible bridge into a structured, step-by-step path from vision to execution.

Strategic Roadmaps for Leaders

If planning is the invisible bridge across the Execution Gap, then **strategic roadmaps are the planks that make that bridge walkable.** They are how leaders turn bold ambitions into navigable steps, how strategy becomes structure, and how teams move forward without falling into chaos.

A compelling vision, no matter how inspiring, achieves nothing unless it's translated into a roadmap. Without one, execution becomes like wandering through a mountain range without trail markers – exhausting, disorienting, and often fatal. With a roadmap, the path is visible, sequential, and actionable.

Why Leaders Struggle with Roadmaps

Despite their importance, roadmaps are often misunderstood or misused. Some leaders **oversimplify**, reducing them to neat slides with "Now, Next, Later." These look elegant but ignore real-world complexity, leaving teams overconfident and underprepared. Others swing to the opposite extreme and **overcomplicate**, burying execution under 200-slide decks packed with micro-tasks and jargon – detail that obscures direction.

Rigidity is another trap. Treating roadmaps as contracts carved in stone discourages adaptation. When conditions change, teams cling to outdated plans, and momentum stalls. A fourth pitfall is **lack of ownership**. Many roadmaps are created centrally and handed down, leaving those tasked with execution feeling no connection to the plan. And finally, some roadmaps are **detached from reality** – they capture aspirations but ignore resource limits, market dynamics, or regulatory hurdles, becoming fantasy maps: beautiful on paper, useless in practice.

Climbing Everest

Climbing Everest without an acclimatization schedule, supply plan, or intermediate camps would end in predictable failure. The summit is the **vision**, but the roadmap is the sequence of camps, climbs, and logistics that make the ascent possible. Climbers don't succeed through ambition alone – they succeed because they respect the roadmap.

The Cascade Model of Roadmapping

A powerful roadmap balances ambition with structure. It cascades vision into increasingly concrete layers:

- **North Star** – The ultimate destination (e.g., "achieve carbon neutrality by 2030").
- **Strategic Themes** – 3–5 big levers that drive the mission (e.g., energy efficiency, supply chain redesign, renewable investments).
- **Initiatives** – Programs that bring themes to life (e.g., retrofitting facilities).
- **Projects** – Specific, accountable actions (e.g., installing smart systems in Plant A).
- **KPIs** – Metrics that track progress (e.g., reducing energy use by 15% annually).

This cascade links every task to the larger purpose. People stop seeing their work as isolated and instead understand how daily actions advance the North Star.

The PACE Roadmap Canvas

The **PACE Roadmap Canvas** makes this cascade actionable. It's a one-page framework with six components:

1. **North Star** – The defining goal.
2. **Themes** – 3–5 strategic pillars.
3. **Initiatives** – Key programs with timelines.
4. **Milestones** – Time-bound checkpoints.
5. **Accountable Owners** – One name per initiative.
6. **KPIs** – Metrics that define success.

The canvas' power is its discipline: it forces leaders to distill ambition into clarity while preventing both oversimplification and overload.

Regional Bank Transformation

A regional bank pursuing digital transformation initially launched dozens of projects simultaneously. The result: chaos. Leadership paused the frenzy and built a roadmap.

- **North Star:** 70% digital adoption in three years.
- **Themes:** mobile-first design, customer education, backend automation.
- **Initiatives:** app relaunch, digital literacy programs.
- **KPIs:** active digital users, service wait times.

The roadmap forced trade-offs – backend systems were prioritized before flashy features. Within three years, adoption soared and customer satisfaction improved.

Why Most Roadmaps Fail

Even well-intentioned roadmaps collapse when they're too broad, listing endless initiatives that overwhelm teams; too rigid, resisting adaptation; or too disconnected, designed far from operational reality.

An NGO's plan to combat child malnutrition in 20 states failed because the roadmap ignored capacity and sequencing. Resources spread too thin, progress stalled, and outcomes faltered. The roadmap became a burden, not a bridge.

The Living Roadmap

The remedy is to treat roadmaps as **living documents** – adaptive guides that evolve with feedback and conditions.

Key principles:

- **Frequency:** Review often – monthly for initiatives, quarterly for themes.
- **Sequencing:** Pace initiatives according to capacity.
- **Feedback:** Link roadmaps to rolling plans and adjust as assumptions shift.
- **Ownership:** Name a single accountable person for every initiative.
- **Communication:** Share updates widely to keep alignment strong.

When leaders follow these principles, roadmaps shift from static artifacts to dynamic execution systems.

Steps to Create Your Strategic Roadmap

1. **Define Your North Star** – Identify the single outcome that defines success.

2. **Select 3–5 Themes** – Focus on what matters most.
3. **Identify Initiatives** – Outline programs with timelines.
4. **Break into Projects** – Assign accountable owners.
5. **Attach KPIs** – Measure progress.
6. **Test Feasibility** – Check against resources and constraints.
7. **Cascade Communication** – Roll it down to all levels and clarify ownership.

Waterfall and Streams

A vision is like a waterfall – powerful but unfocused. A roadmap channels that power into streams that irrigate the right fields. Without channels, water floods randomly and loses force. Roadmaps channel ambition into impact.

Strategic roadmaps are where leadership proves its ability to **translate inspiration into navigation.** They aren't about producing slides – they're about creating shared language, visible priorities, and a structured path to results.

Without them, organizations exhaust themselves in chaos, even when the vision is clear. With them, execution feels inevitable because the bridge is mapped plank by plank.

The next section explores **why roadmaps fail** and how to design systems that balance clarity with adaptability.

Why Most Roadmaps Fail

If roadmaps are the planks that make the bridge of planning walkable, why do so many collapse under the weight of execution? Leaders unveil them with fanfare, yet a year later progress stalls. Teams spend hours building detailed documents, but projects still falter. The issue is rarely the absence of a roadmap – it's that the roadmap itself was flawed in **design, adoption, or evolution.**

Most failures trace back to four predictable traps: **too broad, too rigid, too detached, or too aspirational.** Recognizing and avoiding them is essential if a roadmap is to become a living instrument of execution rather than a ceremonial artifact.

Trap 1: Too Broad – When Focus Is Lost

The most common failure is trying to do everything. In the desire to satisfy all stakeholders, leaders cram every initiative into the plan. On paper it feels inclusive. In practice, it diffuses focus. When everything is a priority, nothing is.

Teams spread thin across dozens of projects, progress slows, and energy drains. Instead of propelling the organization forward, a bloated roadmap weighs it down – like a ship dragging too many anchors.

An FMCG company launched a five-year roadmap with over **60 initiatives** spanning supply chain, marketing, and HR. None reached completion, and employees complained of "initiative overload." The CEO eventually scrapped the plan, admitting that breadth had become the enemy of depth. A roadmap that tries to please everyone ends up serving no one.

Trap 2: Too Rigid – When Plans Resist Reality

Another frequent reason roadmaps fail is rigidity. Leaders treat them as contracts etched in stone, believing that sticking to the plan signals strength. But the world doesn't stand still. Markets shift, regulations change, and technologies disrupt. A rigid roadmap discourages adaptation, trapping teams in outdated actions.

A telecom company began a three-year digital roadmap. Midway, new data-privacy laws emerged, but leadership insisted on following the original plan. Millions were wasted on non-compliant systems before changes were allowed. What was meant to guide execution instead became a liability.

Trap 3: Too Detached – When Plans Are Made in Isolation

Some roadmaps fail because they're created far from the front lines. Senior leaders or consultants design them without ground-level input, then hand them down for execution. On paper, they look brilliant. In practice, they're irrelevant.

Detached roadmaps also erode trust. Teams see them as "their plan," not "our plan," and disengage. Without ownership, even the most elegant roadmap becomes a museum piece – admired but unused.

A manufacturing company's corporate office drafted a sweeping productivity roadmap without consulting plant managers. It ignored aging equipment, local rules, and workforce realities. Execution stalled until managers were brought into **co-create** a revised plan. The first roadmap failed not from lack of intelligence but from lack of intimacy with reality.

Trap 4: Too Aspirational – When Hope Replaces Execution

Some roadmaps collapse because they are more wish list than plan. Leaders declare sweeping goals – "digitally transform every process in two years" – without grounding them in capacity or sequencing. Ambition inspires briefly, but once execution begins, the gap between aspiration and reality becomes painfully clear.

An NGO announced a roadmap to eradicate child malnutrition in **20 states simultaneously**. The bold plan thrilled donors but ignored capacity constraints. Resources spread too thin, initiatives overlapped, and outcomes faltered. Within three years, the roadmap collapsed. The vision was noble, but the plan was a **fantasy map** – inspiring but impractical.

The Failure Equation

These traps combine into a predictable formula:

- **Breadth** spreads teams too thin.
- **Rigidity** locks them into outdated actions.
- **Detachment** alienates ownership.
- **Over-aspiration** raises expectations but delivers disappointment.

Together:
Breadth + Rigidity + Detachment + Aspirations (without grounding) = Roadmap Collapse

Why Leaders Fall Into These Traps

Leaders don't fail out of incompetence but out of bias:

- **Breadth bias:** fear of disappointing stakeholders.
- **Rigidity bias:** belief that sticking to the plan signals strength.
- **Detachment bias:** overconfidence in a top-down perspective.
- **Aspiration bias:** overestimating capability, underestimating constraints.

These instincts are natural – but dangerous. Unless leaders consciously counter them, they design roadmaps destined to fail.

The Path to Roadmaps That Work

Successful roadmaps follow four counter-principles:

- **Focus** counters breadth – prioritize ruthlessly.
- **Adaptability** counters rigidity – treat roadmaps as living guides.
- **Connection** counters detachment – co-create with those who execute.
- **Grounding** counters over-aspiration – anchor ambition in reality.

A healthcare network needed to digitize records across dozens of hospitals. Instead of declaring "digitize everything now," leaders set a North Star of **80% adoption in five years**, piloted in three hospitals, and iterated based on feedback. Co-creation with doctors and administrators ensured connection. Five years later, adoption exceeded 85%. The roadmap succeeded because it avoided all four traps.

The Paper Bridge

A poorly designed roadmap is like a **paper bridge** stretched across a canyon. From afar, it looks convincing. Leaders admire its bold span. But when teams try to cross, it collapses under weight. Strong roadmaps are built of **steel and stone** – focus, adaptability, connection, and grounding – or they cannot carry execution forward.

Roadmaps don't fail because they're unimportant – they fail because they're mishandled. Leaders fall into traps of **breadth, rigidity, detachment, and aspiration**, and the result is wasted effort, broken trust, and widening execution gaps.

But failure is not inevitable. By **focusing, adapting, connecting, and grounding**, leaders can build roadmaps that endure pressure, inspire confidence, and truly carry organizations forward.

The next section explores the **Planning Paradox** – the tension between long-term clarity and short-term unpredictability – and how PACE's approach of MVP planning and rolling plans resolves it.

The Planning Paradox and the PACE Solution

Planning is essential – yet paradoxical. Leaders are told to plan deeply but warned against over-planning. They're urged to set bold long-term goals but also to stay nimble in a volatile world. They're advised to focus resources and prepare for disruption simultaneously.

This tension defines the **Planning Paradox**:

- **Without planning, execution drifts.**
- **With rigid planning, execution suffocates.**

The answer isn't choosing one extreme. It's building a planning discipline that offers both **clarity** and **adaptability**.

The Nature of the Planning Paradox

Leadership operates across two time horizons:

1. **Long-term clarity:** Organizations need a North Star to mobilize resources and inspire belief. Without it, coherence and motivation erode.
2. **Short-term adaptability:** The world shifts constantly – markets evolve, crises strike, competitors innovate. Detailed five-year plans quickly become irrelevant.

The challenge is balancing these forces – providing stability without pretending the future is stable.

A sustainable fashion startup aimed to become top most trusted brand in ten years. But its fixed five-year plan was obsolete within 18 months as trade shifts disrupted supply chains and consumer trends evolved. The founders learned that **long-term vision is necessary – but detailed long-term plans are fantasy**. They shifted to setting a North Star while planning execution in adaptive increments.

Why Traditional Planning Breaks Down

Old-school planning models emerged in predictable, industrial-era markets. Leaders could map five- or ten-year plans with confidence. Today's reality – shaped by digital disruption, geopolitical volatility, and rapid innovation – renders that approach brittle.
What once brought stability now risks locking organizations into outdated paths. Planning itself isn't obsolete – but **how we plan must evolve**.

The PACE Solution: Dual Gears of Planning

The PACE framework resolves the paradox by combining two complementary "gears":

1. **MVP Planning (Minimum Viable Planning)** – for clarity and focus.
2. **Rolling Plans** – for adaptability and continuous recalibration.

Together, they align ambition with agility.

Gear 1: MVP Planning – Focus on the Vital Few

Inspired by the Minimum Viable Product mindset, MVP Planning accelerates execution without drowning in complexity. It focuses on three core questions:

1. What is our **North Star**?
2. What **2–3 initiatives** will move us toward it in the next cycle?
3. **Who owns** each initiative?

Everything else is noise. MVP Planning cuts clutter, concentrates energy, and commits resources to the essential.

An AI chatbot company aspiring to lead customer-service automation resisted the urge to plan five years of features. Instead, it focused on two immediate priorities – multilingual support and CRM integration. Within months, traction and client wins followed. Clarity and speed replaced paralysis.

Gear 2: Rolling Plans – Planning as a Living Practice

Where MVP Planning sets direction, Rolling Plans ensure course correction. Rather than static annual reviews, rolling plans evolve continuously:

- **Short-cycle reviews** (monthly or quarterly).
- **Testing and updating assumptions** as conditions change.
- **Sequencing initiatives** instead of stacking them.
- **Retiring outdated projects** without guilt.

Rolling Plans make planning a rhythm, not an event.

A hospital network digitizing patient records avoided a rigid five-year blueprint. Instead, it adopted rolling quarterly reviews. Pilots led to insights, insights reshaped plans, and adoption climbed steadily past 80%. The organization gained agility without losing sight of the North Star.

The Planning Paradox Matrix

Visualize planning along two axes – **Clarity** and **Adaptability**:

	Low Adaptability	**High Adaptability**
Low Clarity	Drift – no direction, no rhythm.	Chaos – pivots without coherence.
High	Rigidity – brittle plans	**Resilient Execution – the PACE zone.** MVP

Clarity	stuck in the past.	Planning + Rolling Plans

The goal is the top-right quadrant – **high clarity and high adaptability** – where execution thrives.

How to Implement the Dual Gears

Leaders can operationalize MVP Planning and Rolling Plans as a continuous cycle:

1. **Set the North Star** (annually or multi-year) - e.g., "Reduce carbon footprint by 40% in five years."
2. **Define the MVP Plan** (quarterly/semi-annual) - Identify 2–3 key initiatives and assign owners.
3. **Run Rolling Reviews** (monthly/quarterly) - Revisit progress, question assumptions, and adapt.
4. **Renew the MVP Plan** - Replace completed initiatives with new priorities.
5. **Communicate the Rhythm** - Make the cadence visible so teams trust the process.

A renewable-energy company targeting carbon neutrality by 2035 avoided a rigid 15-year plan. Year 1 focused on solarizing HQ and auditing supply-chain emissions. Quarterly reviews revealed new insights, prompting earlier supplier engagement. Over time, MVP Plans evolved – from HQ to plants, suppliers to logistics – sustaining momentum and relevance.

The Human Side: Stability + Flexibility

Beyond mechanics, dual-gear planning meets a deeper psychological need. Teams crave **stability** – a clear destination – but also **flexibility** – confidence that leaders will adapt when reality shifts.

- **MVP Planning provides stability:** "Here's where we're going and what we're doing now."
- **Rolling Plans provide flexibility:** "We'll adjust as we learn."

Together, they build trust. Teams neither feel whiplashed by shifting priorities nor suffocated by rigid plans. Planning becomes a steady rhythm – reliable yet responsive.

Tracks and Switches

Strategy is like a railway journey. **Tracks** (the North Star) set the course; **switches** (Rolling Plans) enable adjustments without derailment. Without tracks, the train meanders. Without switches, it crashes. With both, the journey is purposeful and smooth.

The Planning Paradox is real: without planning, execution drifts; with rigid planning, it suffocates. But leaders need not choose between chaos and control. By adopting PACE's dual-gear solution – **MVP Planning for clarity and Rolling Plans for adaptability** – they transform planning from a one-off exercise into a living discipline.

This approach balances vision with realism, direction with responsiveness, and ambition with execution.

In the next section, we'll examine how **Rolling Plans** differ from fixed roadmaps – and how leaders can institutionalize this rhythm to build organizations that are both stable and agile.

Rolling Plans vs. Fixed Roadmaps – Balancing Agility and Stability

Leaders often feel trapped between two extremes. On one side are **fixed roadmaps** – detailed, rigid, and comforting in their certainty, yet brittle in the face of change. On the other is **constant improvisation** – agile in theory but chaotic in practice. What most organizations truly need is a balance: a system that preserves strategic direction while staying responsive to reality. This is where **rolling plans** come in.

Rolling plans do not discard roadmaps; they evolve them. They preserve the long-term destination but revisit near-term actions regularly, adapting to new information. They transform planning from a static document into a living practice.

Why Fixed Roadmaps Fail

Fixed roadmaps are seductive. They create a sense of control, reassure stakeholders, and make execution look orderly. But beneath that surface lie three fatal flaws.

First, they **assume predictability**. A five-year roadmap imagines a stable future, but markets shift, technologies evolve, and regulations change. By year two, many roadmaps are already outdated.

Second, they **ignore feedback**. Fixed plans are often treated as sacred. Even when evidence shows assumptions were wrong, teams stick to the script. Lessons remain unused, and missteps compound.

Third, they **create rigidity**. Because roadmaps are seen as commitments, altering them can be misread as failure. Leaders hesitate to pivot, and organizations double down on outdated paths.

The result is execution theater: teams march according to the plan simply because it exists, not because it still makes sense.

Why Rolling Plans Succeed

Rolling plans succeed precisely because they address these flaws. They **embrace uncertainty**, **institutionalize feedback**, and **normalize adaptation**. Instead of treating change as disruption, they build it into the system.

The essence of rolling planning is **rhythm**. Leaders commit to reviewing, refining, and renewing plans on a regular cadence – monthly, quarterly, or semi-annually. This creates a powerful paradox: **change becomes predictable**. Teams know plans will evolve, but they also know when and how that evolution will occur.

Rolling plans turn adaptability from a reactive scramble into an organizational habit.

Retail Expansion in Motion

A regional retail chain illustrates the difference between fixed and rolling approaches. Initially, its leaders launched a rigid three-year roadmap to open 50 new stores. But a year later, consumer behavior shifted sharply toward e-commerce. The roadmap, built for physical expansion, suddenly felt obsolete.

Rather than abandoning planning, leadership pivoted to rolling plans. Every quarter, they reviewed data, tested assumptions, and recalibrated priorities. Expansion in some regions slowed, others accelerated, and e-commerce investments were woven into the plan. The long-term ambition – national presence – never changed. But the path to get there evolved continuously.

The results spoke for themselves: within five years, the company achieved its physical expansion targets *and* built a thriving online business. The fixed roadmap would have locked them into irrelevance. Rolling plans kept them agile, adaptive, and aligned.

The Rolling Plan Cycle

Rolling plans can be visualized as a continuous five-stage cycle:

1. **Set Direction**
   - Start with the North Star and high-level themes.
   - Clarify what success looks like over the long term.
2. **Define Near-Term Priorities**
   - Identify two or three initiatives for the next cycle (quarter or half-year).
   - Keep them focused and achievable.
3. **Execute and Monitor**
   - Deliver on initiatives with clear ownership.
   - Track KPIs and gather feedback.
4. **Review and Reflect**
   - At the end of each cycle, assess progress and test assumptions.
   - Celebrate wins and capture lessons.
5. **Renew and Adjust**
   - Update priorities for the next cycle based on insights gained.
   - Retire outdated initiatives and launch new ones.

This cycle repeats indefinitely, enabling organizations to stay both directional and adaptive – anchored to their vision but responsive to reality.

Sailing With the Wind

Think of leadership like captaining a ship across an ocean. A fixed roadmap is plotting every detail before departure – and refusing to adjust when the wind changes. Rolling plans, by contrast, set a destination but adjust the sails regularly. The ship still reaches its destination, but it does so by reading the weather, shifting course, and harnessing changing winds.

The Stability Question

Critics of rolling plans often worry they breed instability: "If plans change every quarter, won't teams feel disoriented?" The answer is no – provided the rhythm is predictable.

Stability does not come from rigidity. It comes from **structure**. When teams know that planning reviews happen on a clear cadence, they trust the process. Change is expected, but it arrives on schedule – guided by evidence, not whims. Rolling plans replace the *false stability* of fixed roadmaps with the *real stability* of structured adaptability.

Building Rolling Plans

Leaders can shift from static roadmaps to rolling plans by following five key practices:

1. **Anchor in a North Star**
   Keep the long-term destination constant. Without it, rolling plans risk devolving into endless pivots.
2. **Define Planning Cycles**
   Choose a review rhythm that matches your environment – quarterly for fast-moving industries, semi-annual for stable ones. Communicate this rhythm clearly.
3. **Limit Active Initiatives**
   Focus each cycle on a small number of priorities. Too many initiatives dilute focus and delay results.
4. **Make Assumptions Explicit**
   Document the assumptions behind every initiative. Revisit and test them at each review cycle.
5. **Create Rituals of Renewal**
   Turn reviews into reflection points. Retire what no longer serves, add what is needed, and reset focus.

These steps transform planning from a static exercise into an evolving system.

Why Rolling Plans Are Hard for Leaders

Despite their advantages, rolling plans require courage. Fixed roadmaps offer the illusion of control; they let leaders feel they have mastered the future. Rolling plans demand humility – the acknowledgment that we cannot know everything in advance.

They also demand cultural maturity. Shifting course can look like indecision unless leaders reframe adaptation as strength. It's not about changing direction impulsively; it's about staying responsive and resilient.

The Train and the Tracks

Leading with rolling plans is like building a railway line as the train moves. The destination remains unchanged, but the track is extended and adjusted as terrain and conditions evolve. This ensures steady progress without derailment – a dynamic system aligned with reality.

Fixed roadmaps provide false certainty. Improvisation breeds chaos. Rolling plans offer a third way – balancing clarity with flexibility, stability with adaptability. They institutionalize rhythm, turning adaptation from a reaction into a capability.

For leaders, this is more than a planning method. It's a mindset shift – one that embraces humility, builds trust, and ensures that plans evolve as fast as the world around them.

The next section will explore how to embed this rhythm into the organization's DNA, making rolling plans not just a leadership tool but a cultural habit that sustains execution over time.

Embedding Rolling Plans into Organizational DNA

Rolling plans are not a tactic. They are not a "tool" leaders deploy during turbulent times and shelve once the storm passes. They are the heartbeat of adaptive organizations – the rhythm that keeps them alive, learning, and leading in a volatile world. Until that rhythm is hardwired into the company's DNA, rolling plans remain fragile. They disappear with leadership changes, collapse under cultural inertia, and fade as soon as stability returns. To unleash their full power, leaders must transform rolling plans from an initiative into an identity.

This is not about adding one more process. It's about rewiring how the organization thinks, decides, learns, and acts. Just as physical strength is built not through a single workout but through disciplined repetition, organizational adaptability is built by embedding rolling plans into the daily, weekly, and quarterly cadence of work – until they become second nature.

Why Rolling Plans Fade – and What It Teaches Us

Most organizations that adopt rolling plans abandon them within a few years. The reasons reveal where real transformation must occur:

- They are treated as **temporary responses** to crises, not as permanent systems. Once the storm calms, old habits return.
- They are never **ritualized** into calendars and cadences. Without predictable cycles, rolling plans devolve into ad hoc reviews.
- They **depend on personalities**. A new CEO with a different style can dismantle them overnight if they're not culturally rooted.
- They are **undermined by fear**. Honest assumption reviews require psychological safety. In low-trust cultures, people hide mistakes instead of surfacing them.

These aren't operational failures – they are cultural and systemic failures. And they underscore a deeper truth: rolling plans succeed not when they are introduced, but when they are embedded.

The Three Layers of Embedding Rolling Plans

Embedding rolling plans into organizational DNA requires action at three levels: systems, culture, and leadership. Each is necessary; none is sufficient alone.

1. Systems Layer – Building Cadence and Rituals

The first step is to make rolling plans unavoidable – not optional. Systems enforce discipline. Leaders must design **cadences** that institutionalize reflection, renewal, and recalibration.

- **Quarterly Business Reviews (QBRs):** Every quarter must include structured reviews of assumptions, outcomes, and priorities. These aren't status updates – they're decision-making forums.
- **Monthly Check-Ins:** Shorter cycles keep momentum alive and surface issues before they become crises.
- **Annual Strategic Resets:** Even with rolling plans, an annual look at the long-term North Star ensures coherence.

These cadences must become as predictable as payroll.

One large conglomerate embedded QBRs into board governance – requiring leadership to present rolling plan updates alongside financials. This single move ensured rolling planning survived multiple CEO transitions because it was no longer a preference; it was a governance expectation.

2. Culture Layer – Making Adaptability a Core Belief

Systems create structure, but **culture gives it soul**. Rolling plans thrive only in cultures where adaptability is seen not as weakness but as strength. That requires rewriting the stories an organization tells about success.

Instead of celebrating leaders who "stuck to the plan," celebrate those who **pivoted intelligently**. Instead of hiding failed assumptions, extract and share the lessons they yield.

A retail chain reshaped its culture by spotlighting "adaptation wins" at company town halls. Teams that identified faulty assumptions early and changed course were publicly honored. The message was clear: agility is not deviation – it is discipline.

3. Leadership Layer – Modeling Renewal from the Top

No system or culture shift endures unless leaders embody it. Rolling plans demand humility and vulnerability – qualities that many executives find uncomfortable. Leaders must be willing to say, "We were wrong," and show how they are revising assumptions.

An energy company's CEO began every quarterly review by sharing one assumption he had personally revised. That vulnerability cascaded downward. Teams began surfacing their own flawed assumptions without fear, transforming reviews from blame sessions into learning sessions. Leaders don't just sponsor rolling plans – they *live* them.

The Rolling Plan Flywheel

When embedded deeply, rolling plans set a self-reinforcing flywheel in motion:

1. **Clarity** - A clear North Star and focused MVP initiatives set direction.
2. **Cadence** - Regular reviews build reflection into the organization's heartbeat.
3. **Adaptation** - Teams pivot early and often, without fear of failure.
4. **Momentum** - Wins accumulate, strengthening belief in the system.
5. **Resilience** - The organization internalizes adaptability as a core strength.

Once this flywheel spins, rolling plans cease to be a "project." They become the default mode of operating.

The Pulse of the Organization

Rolling plans are the organization's pulse. A steady heartbeat sustains life; a disrupted rhythm signals danger. When rolling plan cycles falter, execution weakens, learning slows, and responsiveness fades. Embedding rolling plans is about maintaining that steady pulse – predictable, disciplined, life-sustaining.

The 7-Step Framework for Leaders

To embed rolling plans into the fabric of your organization, follow this roadmap:

1. **Define the Rhythm**
   Choose planning cycles suited to your context – quarterly for dynamic industries, semi-annual for more stable ones.
2. **Integrate into Calendars**
   Bake reviews into organizational calendars alongside financial reporting. Treat them as immovable rituals.
3. **Train Teams on Assumption Mapping**
   Equip teams to identify and articulate the assumptions behind every initiative – and test them systematically.
4. **Build Psychological Safety**
   Create environments where surfacing failed assumptions is rewarded, not punished.
5. **Model Adaptability at the Top**
   Leaders must share their own revised assumptions and pivots publicly.
6. **Reward Adaptation, Not Just Delivery**
   Recognize teams that make intelligent course corrections, not just those that hit original targets.
7. **Cascade the Practice**
   Extend rolling plans beyond strategy – into HR, supply chain, operations, and more – until it becomes the organizational norm.

The Airline That Made Rolling Plans Its DNA

An airline first adopted rolling plans as a survival tactic during volatile fuel price swings. Quarterly assumption reviews helped it respond quickly to shifting conditions. But the breakthrough came when leadership institutionalized the practice across the company. Rolling plans became standard in operations, marketing, and finance – and adaptability was celebrated in newsletters and town halls.

When a new CEO arrived, the system endured because it was no longer tied to a single leader's philosophy – it was part of the airline's identity. Years later, when another crisis hit, the airline outpaced competitors by rapidly adjusting routes, pricing, and staffing. Rolling plans were no longer a project. They were the company's muscle memory.

The Drip, Not the Flood

Embedding rolling plans is not a one-time flood that reshapes everything overnight. It is a steady drip – consistent, patient, and transformative. Over time, that drip wears grooves into the bedrock of culture, shaping how decisions are made and how execution unfolds.

Rolling plans are more than a leadership technique – they are a cultural operating system. They must become the pulse that keeps the organization alive, the reflex that keeps it learning, and the discipline that keeps it adapting.

Embedding them requires more than smart design. It demands systems that enforce rhythm, cultures that celebrate adaptation, and leaders who model renewal. When done well, rolling plans outlive leaders, strategies, and business cycles. They become the organization's immune system – enabling it to absorb shocks, evolve continuously, and sustain execution across generations.

This is the destination of planning maturity: when adaptability ceases to be a response and becomes a reflex. And with that, we are ready to tie the journey together – from invisible scaffolding to living culture – in the closing of this chapter.

Before the Walk: Planning with Purpose

Planning, when done right, is less about documents and more about discipline. It's the quiet architecture that turns ambition into reality. Organizations that endure aren't the loudest – they are the most consistent in planning.

Exceptional leaders don't just declare the future; they prepare their people for it. Planning is that preparation – the invisible force that allows teams to move with clarity even as the path shifts.

The danger lies in extremes. Some see planning as bureaucracy and abandon it, leaving teams adrift. Others treat it as certainty, freezing execution into rigid blueprints. Both miss the point: planning isn't about predicting the future – it's about being ready for it.

PACE reframes planning as a living, breathing discipline – not a yearly ritual, but a leadership rhythm. It shows that clarity and adaptability are not opposites, but partners. When planning is stripped to its essence and revisited regularly, execution becomes resilient. Teams trust both the direction and the process.

In a world where disruption is constant, planning isn't optional. Crises will come, markets will shift, and leaders won't have all the answers. But they can build adaptable systems that stay aligned to the destination. That's the real gift of planning: not certainty, but resilience. Leaders who master this gift leave behind more than results – they build cultures that learn, adapt, and move together. They turn planning into a habit, and strategy into shared action.

The test of leadership is simple: when the winds change, does your organization stumble, or shift its sails with confidence? Planning – living, rolling, and embedded – makes that difference.

"The measure of a leader is not in how firmly they hold the plan, but in how firmly they hold the course."

Pause and Reflect

As you close this chapter, look at the strength of your planning bridge and ask yourself:

- Do I dedicate enough time to planning, or do I dismiss it as "operations work"?
- Where has vision in my organization stalled because the bridge of planning was too weak or absent?
- Are our priorities sequenced with intention, or are we trying to move in all directions at once?
- How visible are ownership, milestones, and risks in our current plans?
- What planning rituals – quarterly reviews, feedback loops, scenario tests – must become part of our leadership rhythm?

Next Step on the Journey

A bridge-builder doesn't boast about the destination; they focus on every plank, bolt, and beam that will carry others across. So must leaders. As you move forward, carry this mindset: **planning is not what delays execution – it's what makes execution possible**. And yet, even the strongest plans mean little without someone willing to stand behind them. That's why the next chapter turns to the force that transforms plans into progress: **accountability**.

CHAPTER THREE

Accountability

The Missing Link Between Strategy and Success

"Accountability is not about blame for the past; it's about ownership of the future."

Why Accountability is the Missing Piece

Organizations rarely stumble because they lack intelligence, ambition, or even a sound strategy. They falter because strategy remains trapped in boardroom slides while execution on the ground unravels. The bridge between vision and results is accountability – and too often, that bridge is weak or missing altogether. Leaders pour resources into off-sites, dashboards, and performance reviews, but when initiatives stall or projects collapse, the diagnosis usually points to technical causes: "We need better systems," "We lacked data," or "We underestimated complexity." These explanations sound reasonable, yet they skirt the deeper truth: without clear ownership, even the best strategies go nowhere.

When no one owns outcomes, strategy becomes theater – impressive to watch, but irrelevant to results.

The Boat That Doesn't Move

Picture a rowing crew where only half the team is pulling while the others barely dip their oars. The boat drifts, progress slows, and frustration builds among those carrying the load. That is what organizations without accountability look like: scattered effort, mounting resentment, and stalled momentum.

A mid-sized technology company learned this the hard way. Despite detailed plans and approved budgets, a major product launch fell apart. Marketing assumed supply chain was driving the schedule. Supply chain assumed product managers were. Product managers assumed leadership was. Everyone believed the plan was someone else's to execute. Progress stalled, competitors surged ahead, and morale plummeted. The problem wasn't the strategy – it was the vacuum of ownership.

Why Strategy Without Accountability Fails

Research confirms that accountability is the critical link between ambition and achievement. The Project Management Institute found that more than 70% of failed initiatives are not the result of poor strategy but of poor execution – and unclear ownership sits at the heart of that gap. A study by Partners in Leadership revealed that only 15% of employees could identify their organization's top three goals, and fewer than half of those knew who was accountable for delivering them. The result is not sabotage but diffusion – responsibility so widely spread that it disappears.

The Hidden Signs of Accountability Gaps

Accountability gaps often masquerade as unrelated problems. Leaders see symptoms but misinterpret their cause. They notice chronic firefighting as teams lurch from crisis to crisis because no one owned prevention. They see blame cycles in which energy is wasted pointing fingers instead of solving problems. Meetings grow silent when leaders ask, "Who owns this?" and no hands rise. Micromanagement creeps in because leaders no longer trust that others will step up. Busywork replaces meaningful outcomes as people confuse activity with progress.

These patterns tempt leaders to tighten control – adding more reports, approvals, and bureaucracy. Ironically, those responses make the problem worse. The tighter the grip, the less ownership people feel, and the more accountability slips away.

Accountability as the Execution Gap

When execution fails, leaders often question the quality of the plan. But most plans fail not because they were flawed, but because no one truly owned them. A brilliant digital roadmap is meaningless if no one owns implementation deadlines. A cost-saving initiative collapses if no one is accountable for enforcing trade-offs. A transformation program stalls if responsibility is diluted across committees. As one executive famously said, "We don't have a strategy problem. We have a follow-through problem."

A pharmaceutical R&D division illustrates the point. Despite significant investment in a breakthrough drug, milestones kept slipping. Researchers blamed regulatory teams, regulatory blamed operations, and operations blamed partners. A new director reframed everything around accountability. Every milestone had a single owner. Decision rights were explicit. Daily huddles surfaced obstacles early. Within 18 months, the drug reached market – not because the science changed, but because ownership did.

Why Accountability Is So Often Missing

If accountability is so essential, why is it so rare? Three reasons explain its absence. First, cultural conditioning: in many organizations, accountability is synonymous with blame. People associate it with punishment, not empowerment. Second, the illusion of shared responsibility: teams assume that "collective accountability" works, but in reality, what belongs to everyone belongs to no one. Finally, leadership blind spots: leaders often mistake control for accountability, inserting themselves into details instead of building ownership.

Until accountability is reframed as empowerment rather than punishment, it will remain elusive.

Diagnosing Accountability Gaps

Leaders can spot accountability breakdowns by asking simple but revealing questions:

- For every missed deliverable, who was the single accountable person?
- Do phrases like "We thought they would handle it" or "That wasn't my role" surface in conversations?
- Are decisions logged with clear names attached?
- Do leaders get dragged into details repeatedly – a sign that ownership is weak below them?

- Does silence follow the question "Who owns this?"

These questions often reveal that what looks like systemic underperformance is really accountability diffusion.

From Blame to Ownership

Closing this gap requires reframing accountability as a force for success, not a tool for punishment. When ownership is clear, people move with confidence. When it's diffuse, even the smartest strategies collapse. Accountability is not one pillar among many – it is the keystone that locks the execution arch together. Without it, everything else wobbles.

The Symptoms of an Accountability Deficit

Accountability gaps rarely arrive with flashing warnings. They slip in quietly, camouflaged as busyness, processes, or well-intentioned activity. Leaders often misinterpret these signs, mistaking motion for progress and compliance for ownership. Over time, the absence of accountability corrodes execution, erodes trust, and breeds a culture where people show up but don't truly step up.

The first defense is awareness. Yet most leaders misdiagnose what they're seeing and respond with the wrong medicine – more reports, more bureaucracy, more oversight – when the real cure is clearer ownership.

The Seven Signals of a Missing Ownership Culture

1. Chronic Firefighting

When no one is accountable upstream, organizations are trapped in reactive mode. Teams rush from one crisis to the next, patching issues instead of preventing them. At a consumer goods company, millions were lost each year fixing last-minute packaging errors. Quality assumed marketing was responsible, marketing assumed operations, and operations assumed suppliers. Without a single owner, fire drills became business as usual. The chaos wasn't complexity – it was missing accountability.

2. Checklist Obsession

When ownership is unclear, activity replaces achievement. Teams focus on ticking boxes rather than delivering results. A financial services firm launching a new compliance system saw each department complete its assigned tasks, yet deadlines slipped and regulators rejected the outcome as incomplete. Everyone had done their part, but no one owned the whole. Busyness had been mistaken for progress.

3. Blame Cycles

In accountability-deficient cultures, failure triggers finger-pointing instead of root-cause diagnosis. A fast-growing tech startup faced weeks of stalemate after a product crash: developers blamed QA, QA blamed operations, and operations blamed leadership. Nothing changed but morale, which sank under the weight of blame. Without ownership, mistakes repeat rather than teach.

4. Silence in Meetings

One of the most revealing signs of weak accountability is silence. When leaders ask, "Who owns this?" and no one answers, it signals fear, confusion, or apathy. That silence is not neutral – it's corrosive. Over time, it becomes silence in execution too, as people hesitate to claim responsibility or make decisions.

5. Micromanagement

Ironically, leaders often respond to low accountability by tightening control. They hover over details, second-guess decisions, and take over tasks. It feels like leadership but signals distrust. A regional retail chain saw soaring manager turnover because district leaders micromanaged every choice, crushing autonomy and discouraging initiative. Low trust bred more micromanagement, which shrank ownership even further.

6. Diffusion of Responsibility

When accountability is spread too thin, it disappears altogether. "Shared responsibility" sounds noble but often means no one owns the outcome. A government IT project assigned to five agencies "collectively" collapsed in integration. Each produced reports, but deadlines slipped for years. A later inquiry revealed the truth: what belonged to everyone belonged to no one.

7. Metrics Without Owners

Dashboards glow with KPIs, yet no names are attached. Goals float as "organizational priorities," but when performance falters, no one feels responsible. At a private bank, client conversion rates plunged 20%, yet silence followed the question, "Who owns this?" Marketing pointed to sales, sales to operations, and operations to strategy. Visibility wasn't the problem – ownership was.

Why Leaders Misread the Signals

These symptoms are often mistaken for problems of effort, competence, or resources. Leaders respond with the wrong tools: more meetings, more reports, more approvals. But these are surface fixes. They add layers of noise without touching the root cause: the absence of clear, lived accountability. Until ownership is clarified and claimed, none of the additional systems will deliver results.

Diagnosing an Accountability Deficit

Leaders can pinpoint accountability gaps with a simple diagnostic approach:

- **Map the Symptoms:** Identify where firefighting, silence, or blame cycles appear most often.
- **Trace Ownership:** For each symptom, ask who the single accountable person was. If no answer emerges, the gap is clear.
- **Listen for Language:** Phrases like "We thought they would..." or "That's not my role" signal ownership voids.
- **Test for Duplication:** Look for overlapping work with no clear leader – a sign of diffusion.
- **Connect to Outcomes:** For every missed KPI, ask who felt ultimate responsibility.

This exercise often reveals that what appears to be systemic underperformance is really systemic ownership absence.

When Leaders Get It Right

A fast-growing SaaS company experienced every symptom during a major product release: firefighting, micromanagement, silence in meetings. Leadership's first instinct was to tighten control – introducing new reporting tools, stricter approvals, and mandatory status updates. But execution slowed further, frustration grew, and talent attrition rose. Only when the CEO reframed accountability – assigning single owners to each module, empowering teams with autonomy, and linking KPIs to names – did the spiral reverse. The release succeeded, and employee satisfaction rebounded.

Symptoms are not the disease, but they are the warning lights on the dashboard. Leaders who interpret them correctly avoid adding more noise to noisy systems. The next step is deeper: reframing accountability itself – shifting it from a tool of blame to a practice of empowerment. That transformation begins in the next section.

Accountability ≠ Blame – Reframing the Concept

The very word *accountability* still makes many employees flinch. For decades, it has been wielded like a weapon – brandished when things go wrong, when mistakes demand scapegoats, or when leaders want to assert control. No wonder it carries a negative charge. But accountability, in its truest form, isn't about punishment. It's about ownership. It's not backward-looking, obsessed with who failed, but forward-looking, focused on who will step up. Unless leaders consciously reframe it away from blame, attempts to build a culture of ownership will backfire. People will retreat, hide mistakes, and resist responsibility. The challenge is to shift accountability from a fear-driven term into an empowerment-driven practice.

The Cost of Blame Cultures

Blame corrodes organizations from the inside out. It distorts behavior, stifles initiative, and erodes performance. Fear of exposure discourages risk-taking, while information hoarding delays responses. Energy is spent protecting reputations instead of advancing outcomes, and high performers leave environments where accountability feels toxic.

A large insurance company learned this lesson the hard way. Repeated project delays triggered witch-hunt postmortems in which leaders demanded to know "who was at fault." Teams arrived prepared with defenses instead of insights. Nothing changed because everyone focused on survival, not solutions. A new leader broke the cycle by asking one simple question: "What did we learn?" The tone shifted, lessons surfaced, collaboration returned, and within a year, delays dropped and innovation accelerated. Blame stifles learning. Ownership accelerates it.

From Punishment to Promise

True accountability is best understood not as a mechanism of punishment but as a promise – a commitment people make to themselves and to others. In a blame mindset, the message is, *"You failed, and now you will be punished."* In an ownership mindset, it becomes, *"I gave my word, and I will honor it."* Seen this way, accountability stops being a burden and becomes aspirational. People feel proud – not pressured – to uphold their commitments.

Language is often the clearest signal of whether accountability is rooted in blame or ownership. Phrases like "Who messed this up?" or "We need to find out who dropped the ball" betray a blame culture. Ownership-driven organizations ask, "What did we learn?" or "Who will take this forward?" That subtle shift in phrasing reflects a profound shift in culture.

A cooperative bank illustrates the point. Compliance failures repeatedly triggered public shaming and punitive reviews, so managers began hiding risks until they became crises. A new COO banned blame language and reframed conversations around commitments: What did we promise? Where did we fall short, and why? How do we recommit? Within a year, compliance issues fell by 40%, and managers surfaced problems early rather than burying them.

Shifting the Culture

Most organizations exist somewhere along a spectrum: at one pole, accountability is toxic – fear-driven, backward-looking, and focused on punishment, producing silence and disengagement. At the other, it is healthy – pride-driven, forward-looking, and centered on commitments, producing openness and resilience. The leader's task is to move the culture decisively toward the latter.

Three shifts accelerate that transition:

- From *"Who is at fault?"* to *"What did we learn?"* – transforming postmortems into learning labs.
- From *"Why didn't you..."* to *"How will we..."* – shifting energy from blame to solutions.
- From *"I have to..."* to *"I own this."* – helping teams frame responsibility as agency.

A manufacturing plant offers a vivid example. Daily quality defects once triggered public blame sessions. Supervisors berated operators, fear spread, and workers began hiding minor issues – which grew into major failures. A new plant head replaced blame with "failure huddles" focused solely on improving the system.

Operators started suggesting fixes, managers stopped shaming individuals, and defect rates fell by 30% in six months. Accountability transformed from punishment into shared improvement.

Mirror, Not Hammer

Accountability is not a hammer to strike people when they stumble; it is a mirror held up so individuals and teams can see their commitments clearly. The hammer creates fear and resistance. The mirror creates awareness, self-correction, and pride. Leaders must choose: will accountability be the hammer that shatters initiative, or the mirror that builds ownership?

Reframing accountability as ownership rather than blame sets the stage for growth. But reframing alone is not enough. Teams need a shared language and structure to climb from excuses to ownership. That is the purpose of the next section: *Ladder of Accountability: The PACE Way.*

Ladder of Accountability: The PACE Way

Reframing accountability as ownership rather than blame is a powerful first step – but it's not enough on its own. Leaders also need a shared model that turns the idea of accountability into a visible, practical journey. Without a framework, accountability remains abstract; people may nod in agreement yet still struggle to understand what ownership looks like in action.

That's where the **Ladder of Accountability: The PACE Way** comes in. This simple yet transformative model helps individuals and teams diagnose where they stand, recognize the behaviors that hold them back, and chart a clear path upward – from denial and deflection at the bottom to full ownership and leadership at the top. Each rung represents a distinct mindset, and as people climb, energy shifts from avoidance to action.

The Seven Rungs of PACE Way Accountability

Every organization has people scattered across these seven rungs. The higher the average rung, the faster execution moves.

1. **Denial – "There is no problem."**
   Individuals refuse to acknowledge issues, insisting nothing is wrong. (*"That's not happening."*)

2. **Blame – "It's someone else's fault."**
   Responsibility is deflected outward. (*"They dropped the ball."*)

3. **Excuses – "I couldn't because..."**
   External factors become shields for inaction. (*"We didn't have enough resources."*)

4. **Wait & See – "Maybe someone else will step in."**
   People hesitate, waiting for others to act. (*"Let's see what leadership decides."*)

5. **Acknowledgment – "Yes, there's an issue."**
   Problems are recognized, though not yet owned. (*"We need to fix this."*)

6. **Ownership – "I will take responsibility."**
   Individuals step forward. (*"I own this – here's how I'll fix it."*)

7. **Execution Leadership – "I drive outcomes and model accountability."**
   Ownership extends beyond personal tasks to shaping accountability in others. (*"Here's the plan, who owns what, and how we'll track progress."*)

As organizations climb higher on the ladder, energy flows into execution instead of excuses. Projects accelerate, problems surface sooner, and learning compounds.

A Tale of Two Mindsets

Ravi and Asha are two product managers leading different modules in a major product release. Just two weeks before launch, a critical integration test failed – a delay would cost millions and damage credibility.

Ravi's instinct was denial. "This isn't my module," he insisted. When evidence showed otherwise, he shifted into blame. "If QA had tested this earlier, we wouldn't be here." Then came excuses: "We didn't have the right documentation." Finally, he defaulted to wait-and-see: "Let's see what leadership decides." Ravi stayed trapped in the lower rungs, reacting defensively and waiting for others to solve the problem. His team mirrored his mindset. Fixes were delayed, momentum stalled, and Ravi's credibility suffered.

Asha faced the same crisis but responded differently. She began with acknowledgment: "Yes, my module has a bug, and it's affecting integration." She then claimed ownership: "I'll pull in a cross-functional team today to isolate and fix it." And she climbed to execution leadership: "Here's the plan, here's who owns each part, and here's how we'll report back." Her clarity and action galvanized her team. The issue was resolved in days, the launch stayed on track, and Asha's leadership reputation grew.

The difference wasn't competence or context – it was the rung they chose to stand on.

Listening for Clues: Language as a Mirror

Leaders can often diagnose where their teams stand simply by listening.

- **Denial, Blame, Excuses:** language is defensive, past-focused, and externalized.
- **Wait & See:** tone is passive and unclear.
- **Acknowledgment, Ownership, Execution:** speech is forward-looking and internalized.

In meetings, capture recurring phrases. Do people say "They didn't tell us" – or "Here's what we can do next"? These linguistic signals reveal cultural norms more accurately than any survey.

How to Help Teams Climb the Ladder

Climbing the ladder requires both **self-awareness** and **system reinforcement**. Leaders play a pivotal role in guiding that journey:

1. **Call Out Denial and Blame Early** – Ask, "What part of this can we control?" and redirect focus to action.
2. **Interrupt Excuses with Curiosity** – Challenge limiting narratives: "What could we do differently despite those constraints?"
3. **Break the Wait & See Loop** – Set clear deadlines and push for proposed solutions.
4. **Reinforce Acknowledgment** – Praise early recognition of problems as a step toward progress.
5. **Model Ownership** – Say "I own this" publicly when things go wrong.
6. **Promote Execution Leadership** – Encourage high performers to mentor others in accountability.

A tech service company applied the PACE Ladder to diagnose why decisions lagged and innovation had slowed. They found most middle managers stuck between *excuses* and *wait & see*. The CEO launched ladder training workshops where teams mapped past responses to rungs and began every project meeting with one question: "Who owns this?" Within six months, decision-making sped up, milestones were consistently met, and engagement scores rose.

Self-Diagnosis and Daily Reinforcement

Teams can also use the ladder as a mirror. Ask: *When faced with a setback, is my first instinct to deny, blame, excuse, wait, acknowledge, own, or lead? What phrases do I use most often? When did I last say "I own this"?* This simple reflection surfaces unconscious habits and sparks change.

Leaders can reinforce accountability through rituals that embed the ladder into daily life:

- **The Ownership Question:** Begin meetings with "Who owns this?"
- **The Language Audit:** Track recurring phrases and map them to rungs.
- **Accountability Storytelling:** Celebrate moments when someone climbed from excuses to ownership.
- **Ladder Visuals:** Display the ladder where teams meet as a constant cue.

Climbing the Mountain

Think of accountability as a mountain climb. At the base, denial and blame form a fog where progress is impossible. As teams climb, acknowledgment clears the air, ownership provides footing, and execution leadership marks the summit – where leaders not only reach the peak but help others climb too. Teams that live in the fog remain lost. Those that climb gain momentum, confidence, and altitude.

The PACE Ladder turns accountability from an abstract principle into a living practice. It helps leaders diagnose reality, teams measure progress, and organizations build a shared language of ownership. But even with ladders, organizations can still stumble if they confuse systems with ownership. That's the next trap – the *accountability illusion.*

The Accountability Illusion – Why Systems Fail

Many organizations believe they've solved the accountability challenge once they've implemented the right systems – dashboards, compliance trackers, automated reminders, cascading reports. These structures look impressive. They create a sense of order. Yet more often than not, they produce an illusion of accountability rather than its reality.

The illusion works like this: metrics are tracked, reports are filed, dashboards glow green – and still, outcomes don't improve. Projects stall. Customers remain unsatisfied. Execution lags. The system measures activity, but no one feels responsible for results. Leaders assume accountability exists because the structure looks neat. Teams disengage because ownership has been outsourced to software and bureaucracy.

True accountability cannot be coded into dashboards or delegated to processes. It must live inside people.

The Shiny Cage

Systems without ownership are like shiny cages: polished, sophisticated – and stifling. They trap energy instead of unleashing it.

A private bank invested millions in a state-of-the-art risk dashboard. Managers dutifully fed it charts and updates, and executives took comfort in weekly reports. But a surprise regulatory audit uncovered major gaps. The issue wasn't data quality – it was absent ownership. No one felt responsible for addressing the risks; teams were reporting, not resolving. The dashboard measured activity but never motivated action.

Why Systems Alone Fail

Even the most sophisticated structures falter without ownership because:

- **They track, not transform.** Dashboards capture what happened but rarely inspire the will to change it.
- **They shift responsibility upward.** As reports climb the hierarchy, ownership is displaced: "Leadership has the data, so they must own the problem."
- **They reward appearance, not action.** Teams polish metrics to stay "green" rather than tackling issues honestly.
- **They create false security.** Leaders see reports and assume progress, while little changes beneath the surface.

The Factory vs. the Garden

Systems-driven accountability treats organizations like factories – feed data in, process it, output compliance. It assumes that if the system is rigid enough, people will fall in line. But accountability behaves more like a garden. It requires cultivation: seeding ownership, watering trust, pruning excuses, creating conditions for growth. You cannot automate a garden into flourishing – you must nurture it. Leaders who mistake factories for gardens end up with compliant processes but disengaged people.

A major retail chain learned this firsthand. Facing falling conversion rates, it launched a dashboard tracking 25 KPIs per store. Managers spent hours feeding data, yet frontline teams felt lost. No one knew what mattered most, and ownership evaporated. A new executive scrapped the complexity and rallied everyone around one North Star metric: conversion. Managers became fully accountable for outcomes, teams experimented locally, and lessons – not just numbers – were reported. Nine months later, conversion rates rose, engagement improved, and reporting time dropped by 40%. Accountability shifted from compliance to ownership.

Spotting the Illusion

Leaders can detect when they're trapped in the illusion by watching for these warning signs:

- **Green dashboards, red outcomes.** Metrics look fine, but performance, revenue, or satisfaction remain stagnant.
- **Volume over value.** Teams spend more time reporting than solving.
- **"We reported it" replaces "We fixed it."** Documentation substitutes for resolution.
- **Meetings review numbers, not commitments.** Discussions stay abstract, and no one leaves owning the next step.

Breaking the Illusion

Escaping the illusion requires leaders to go beyond tracking systems and intentionally build ownership cultures. Four shifts matter most:

1. **From Reporting to Conversation** – Replace static reviews with dialogue: "What are we learning? What will we change?"
2. **From Metrics to North Star** – Focus on the few outcomes that matter most and assign clear owners.

3. **From Compliance to Commitment** – Ask teams to state commitments aloud; people honor promises more than data points.
4. **From Polishing to Problem-Solving** – Stop rewarding "green" reports; reward candor and corrective action.

A technology company believed its quarterly reports were proof of accountability – customer satisfaction hovered above 80%. Yet churn soared. Managers had been massaging scores to avoid punishment. Leadership flipped the model: satisfaction stopped being a punitive metric, "customer commitment reviews" replaced static reports, and teams were praised for surfacing problems early. Within a year, churn declined, and issues surfaced faster. Accountability returned because ownership, not optics, was rewarded.

A Leadership Practice, Not a Process

Systems can support accountability, but they cannot substitute for it. Dashboards and reports create visibility – not responsibility. Real accountability is lived, not logged. It is found not in the neatness of reporting lines but in the clarity of commitments people make and the pride with which they keep them.

The next step is to translate this principle into practice – to build daily rhythms and rituals that make accountability self-sustaining. That's where the **Accountability Action Framework™** comes in.

The Accountability Action Framework™

Awareness is not enough. Leaders can reframe accountability as ownership and diagnose where it's missing – but without a structured way to turn that awareness into daily practice, accountability slips back into theory. Organizations nod along in workshops, but when the real work begins, old habits return: excuses, silences, blame cycles, and dashboards masking disengagement.

The **Accountability Action Framework™** bridges that gap. It is a five-step model that translates the philosophy of accountability into behaviors, systems, and rituals. Think of it as the operating system for ownership – one that works not just for executives but for every layer of the enterprise.

Its five steps build on one another:

1. Surface the Invisible
2. Climb the Ladder
3. Map the Dual System
4. Build the Loop
5. Embed with Rituals

Individually, each step strengthens execution. Together, they transform culture.

Step 1: Surface the Invisible

Most accountability gaps are not hidden because they're complex – they're hidden because no one names them. Missed deadlines get rationalized as "resource constraints." Failed projects are dismissed as "bad luck." Customer complaints are treated as "exceptions." But these are often signals of missing ownership.

Surfacing the invisible means bringing these gaps into the open and making them specific and discussable.

How leaders can do it:

- **Trace backwards:** For every missed outcome, ask, "Who was the single accountable person?" If no clear answer emerges, the gap is real.
- **Spot silences:** Pay attention when "Who owns this?" is met with silence or vague mentions of "the team." Silence is a warning sign.
- **Listen for avoidance:** Phrases like "We assumed they would..." or "That wasn't in our scope" reveal diffusion.

A consulting firm plagued by chronic project overruns blamed complexity and shifting client demands – until leaders traced missed deliverables and found that 40% lacked a named owner. Once surfaced, conversations shifted from excuses to clarity, and delivery times improved.

Accountability gaps are like fog – teams sense something's wrong but can't see the road ahead. Surfacing them is switching on the headlights.

Step 2: Climb the Ladder

Once gaps are visible, the next task is to help people climb from excuses to ownership. The **Ladder of Accountability - PACE Way** shows the path – from denial ("There is no problem") to execution leadership ("I own this and model it for others").

How leaders guide the climb:

- **Diagnose the rung:** Listen for language that signals denial, blame, excuses, or passive waiting.
- **Redirect conversations:** Shift from blame to action ("What's in our control?"), from excuses to possibilities ("What can we still do?"), and from waiting to commitment ("What step will you own now?").
- **Model the climb:** Admit your own mistakes openly – showing that acknowledgment is strength, not weakness.

At a consumer-goods company, managers blamed supply-chain delays for missed sales. A new VP introduced ladder workshops, asking teams to analyze their own language. Most realized they were stuck between "excuses" and "wait and see." Awareness sparked action, and delivery rates improved by 20% – without any new systems, just stronger ownership.

At the base of the mountain, denial and blame live in fog. Ownership is the summit, where clarity and decisive action reside. Leaders don't helicopter teams to the top – they guide the climb.

Step 3: Map the Dual System

Accountability cannot rest solely on individuals; it must be built into the system. But systems alone create bureaucracy unless balanced with ownership. The solution is a **dual system** that integrates:

- **Top-Down Clarity:** Leadership sets the vision, defines the North Star, and clarifies decision rights. Without it, ownership diffuses.
- **Bottom-Up Ownership:** Teams own contextual execution. Without it, accountability suffocates under micromanagement.

A retailer's digital transformation stalled because headquarters dictated every detail. Local teams disengaged, viewing it as "head-office work." Leadership reset the balance: HQ defined the *why* – strategic outcomes and metrics – while stores owned the *how* – adapting solutions locally. Adoption accelerated, innovation increased, and accountability became shared rather than imposed.

In the Rowing Team of Dual System, the coxswain (leader) sets rhythm and direction – top-down clarity. The rowers (teams) supply energy and precision – bottom-up ownership. Without both, the boat stalls.

Leader's roadmap:

1. Define the North Star.
2. Clarify decision rights.
3. Give teams local adaptation room.
4. Build upward feedback loops.

Step 4: Build the Loop

Even with systems in place, accountability decays without feedback. Without loops, commitments vanish. With them, they recycle into learning.

The Four-Part Loop:

1. **Commit** – State commitments clearly and publicly.
2. **Act** – Execute with ownership attached.
3. **Review** – Candidly assess: Did we deliver?
4. **Learn** – Extract lessons and apply them forward.

A pharmaceutical company's rollout struggled despite clear goals. Leaders introduced daily 15-minute huddles where owners declared commitments, reviewed outcomes, and shared learnings. Adoption surged, delays vanished – not because of new tools, but because tight feedback loops kept ownership alive.

Feedback loops are compasses. Without them, teams drift. With them, they continuously adjust course and reach their destination.

Step 5: Embed with Rituals

The final step is making accountability part of the culture. Rituals embed ownership into the organization's muscle memory.

Examples of powerful rituals:

- **The Ownership Question:** Begin meetings with "Who owns this?"
- **Failure Fridays:** Share one mistake and one lesson weekly.
- **Recognition Rounds:** Celebrate acts of ownership, not just outcomes.
- **Accountability Story Vaults:** Retell stories of ownership wins to shape cultural memory.

A startup plagued by missed deadlines introduced daily "ownership check-ins," where every team member declared one deliverable, they would own that day. Within weeks, on-time delivery soared to 90%. The change wasn't just procedural – it was cultural.

Rituals are campfires. Commitment is the spark, systems are the wood, and culture is the flame. Leaders must keep feeding the fire.

The Accountability Action Framework transforms accountability from a lofty principle into a lived practice. But even the most committed individuals and teams need systems that scale – balancing structure and empowerment, strategy and culture. That's the next step: designing **dual accountability systems** that sustain ownership at every level.

Designing Dual Accountability Systems

Accountability is not a solo act. It doesn't reside solely in the willpower of an individual or the charisma of a leader. It lives – or dies – in the system. Even the most motivated people will fail if the system is misaligned. Conversely, when systems dominate without individual ownership, organizations devolve into compliance machines – full of reports, checklists, and approvals, yet barren of real outcomes.

The paradox is clear: accountability thrives only when systems and individuals share it. This is the essence of **dual accountability systems** – designs where top-down clarity and bottom-up ownership reinforce one another. If one side overpowers the other, dysfunction follows. Too much control breeds paralysis. Too much autonomy breeds chaos. The craft of leadership lies in balancing both.

Why Organizations Tilt Off Balance

To design balanced systems, leaders must first understand why imbalance occurs so easily.

Why Leaders Over-Index on Control

- **Fear of Failure:** Leaders cling to approvals and oversight to shield themselves from reputational risk.
- **Illusion of Control:** Dashboards and sign-offs *feel* like control, even when they don't change outcomes.

- **Status Preservation:** Hierarchies often conflate authority with accountability, even when execution should live deeper in the organization.

Why Teams Default to Passivity

- **Cultural Conditioning:** Years of top-down management teach people to wait for direction.
- **Fear of Risk:** Ownership feels dangerous if mistakes are punished.
- **Ambiguity:** Without clarity on decision rights, teams hesitate, unsure where their authority begins.

At the root of these patterns is the **fear–respect dynamic**. Fear-driven accountability produces compliance but kills initiative. Respect-driven accountability produces ownership even in uncertainty. Leaders must actively replace fear with trust – making it safe for people to claim accountability without permission.

A healthcare system learned this the hard way. Nurses consistently underreported safety issues, not out of negligence, but fear. Years of top-down blame had conditioned silence. Leadership flipped the dynamic: managers were retrained to respond with curiosity, not criticism, and dual systems were introduced – national safety standards set top-down clarity, while local teams gained autonomy to escalate issues. Safety reporting soared tenfold, and patient outcomes improved dramatically.

The Anatomy of Dual Accountability

Dual accountability rests on two interdependent pillars:

- **Top-Down Clarity:** Leaders define the "why," set North Star metrics, and draw non-negotiable boundaries. Decision rights are explicit, and values are clearly communicated.
- **Bottom-Up Ownership:** Teams own the "how" – adapting, innovating, and solving problems in context. Feedback flows upward to inform future decisions.

Think of this as a **suspension bridge**. The towers (clarity) keep the bridge stable; the cables (ownership) carry the weight. Remove either, and the bridge collapses.

Failure Modes of Imbalance

When the two pillars fall out of balance, three failure patterns emerge:

1. **Command & Control:** Endless approvals, rigid processes, and disengaged employees. Execution slows because thinking stops.
2. **Chaos:** Excessive autonomy leads to fragmentation, duplication, and inconsistency. Energy is wasted, and scale is lost.
3. **The Vacuum:** Leaders assume teams will lead; teams assume leaders will clarify. Confusion, drift, and finger-pointing follow.

A government agency launching a digital portal fell into this vacuum. Headquarters assumed departments would act; departments assumed HQ would guide. Progress stalled. When accountability was redesigned – HQ owning policy outcomes and departments owning implementation – momentum returned and the portal launched successfully.

A Five-Step Guide for Dual Accountability

To design dual accountability systems, leaders must engineer both structure and psychology. Here's how:

1. Clarify the North Star

Strip complexity down to a single, measurable outcome.

- **Instead of:** "Improve satisfaction, reduce complaints, cut costs, digitize processes."
- **Say:** "Achieve 90% digital adoption in 12 months."

Leader Script: "Here is our North Star. Everything else supports this. If trade-offs arise, this is the measure we protect."

2. Map Decision Rights

Use tools like RACI – but simplify them. Every major deliverable should have **one accountable owner**.

- **Do:** "Store managers are accountable for in-store conversions."
- **Avoid:** Committees as "accountable" – shared accountability is no accountability.

Leader Script: "Who is accountable? Just one name. Who executes? Who do we consult? Who do we inform?"

3. Empower Local Adaptation

Grant teams freedom to decide *how* they meet the North Star, within clear guardrails.

- **Guardrails:** "Compliance rules must never be compromised."
- **Autonomy:** "Each plant may redesign workflows to meet quality targets."

Leader Script: "Here are the guardrails: safety, compliance, and ethics. Within these, you own the how. Surprise us with your ideas."

4. Create Feedback Loops

Regular forums keep accountability alive.

- Weekly check-ins tie outcomes to names.
- Dashboards display progress alongside ownership.
- Learning audits focus on insights, not punishment.

Leader Script: "We're not here to punish. We're here to learn. What worked? What didn't? What will you own next?"

5. Model Accountability at the Top

Nothing erodes accountability faster than leaders who demand it but don't demonstrate it.

- Admit mistakes publicly.
- Share lessons openly.
- Take visible ownership of failures.

Leader Script: "This delay is on me. I didn't clarify priorities. Here's how I'll do better – and here's what I still expect from you."

Accountability is like a seesaw. One side is clarity, the other ownership. Lean too far either way, and balance collapses. Leadership is about holding the center – adjusting weight and momentum so both sides work together.

Dual Accountability in Practice

A leading manufacturer suffered chronic downtime because maintenance accountability was unclear. HQ demanded reports, plants complied, but no one acted. Leaders redesigned the system: HQ owned uptime as a global KPI, plants owned the *how*, and supervisors were named accountable for execution. Weekly feedback loops surfaced issues without blame. Downtime fell 28% in a year. The shift didn't just clarify roles – it rewired psychology. Supervisors stopped waiting, and HQ stopped micromanaging.

Designing dual accountability systems is not about checklists and charts. It's about psychology and balance – replacing fear with trust, clarity with suffocation, and autonomy with abdication. When top-down clarity and bottom-up ownership work in harmony, accountability becomes the bridge between vision and results.

But systems alone don't make accountability resilient. To embed it deeply into culture, leaders need one final layer: feedback loops and rituals that make accountability habitual. That is the focus of the next section.

Building the Loop and Embedding Rituals

Even the best-designed accountability systems decay over time. Attention drifts, momentum fades, and old habits creep back in. That's why the final layer of the **Accountability Action Framework™** is not about introducing new tools – it's about reinforcing accountability so deeply that it becomes self-sustaining.

Two mechanisms achieve this: **feedback loops** and **rituals**. Loops continuously renew accountability through cycles of commitment and learning. Rituals hardwire accountability into the culture by embedding it into daily rhythms. Together, they turn accountability from a project into a way of life.

Why Loops and Rituals Matter

Human beings don't thrive in straight lines – we thrive in cycles. Our lives are built around rhythms: daily routines, weekly reviews, seasonal resets. Cultures form not from one-time declarations but from repeated actions that become norms. Accountability is no different. It cannot be maintained through annual speeches or quarterly reviews. It needs loops that recycle commitments into learning and rituals that transform ownership into habit. Without these reinforcements, organizations relapse into excuses, blame, and silence.

Part I: Building the Loop

A **loop** is not another meeting. It is a design principle — a recurring sequence of **commit → act → review → learn → recommit**. When done right, loops become engines of momentum rather than bureaucratic rituals.

The Four-Part Accountability Loop

1. **Commit** - Individuals or teams make clear, time-bound commitments with visible ownership.
2. **Act** - Execution follows, guided by clarity about who owns what.
3. **Review** - Outcomes are examined candidly: Did we deliver? Did ownership hold?
4. **Learn** - Lessons are distilled and applied to the next cycle.

Without the "learn" step, loops degrade into performance reviews. With it, they become growth systems.

A leading pharmaceutical company discovered this firsthand during a major software rollout. Despite strong systems, adoption lagged. The breakthrough wasn't another dashboard — it was a daily 15-minute loop. Each owner declared commitments, reviewed results, and shared one learning. Within three months, adoption surged and delays vanished. The loop transformed accountability from a static plan into a living, self-correcting practice.

How Leaders Build Effective Loops

- **Tighten the cycle.** Quarterly reviews are too slow. Weekly or daily loops keep accountability alive and feedback immediate.
- **Name names.** Replace vague statements like "the team missed the deadline" with "this owner missed — here's why and how we fix it."
- **Normalize red flags.** If every review is "green," the team is living in illusion. Red signals should spark problem-solving, not punishment.
- **Close the learning loop.** Every review should end with one question: "What will we do differently next time?"

Feedback loops are like compasses. Even with the best maps, teams drift without them. With loops, they continually adjust course, ensuring they arrive where they intend.

Part II: Embedding Rituals

If loops are about correction, **rituals** are about culture. They are symbolic acts repeated until they shape identity. Rituals make accountability instinctive – something people *are*, not just something they *do*.

Why rituals work:

- **Repetition builds culture.** What gets repeated, sticks.
- **Symbolism reinforces values.** Rituals communicate what the organization truly cares about.
- **Participation drives ownership.** Rituals make accountability collective, not imposed.

A fast-scaling tech startup consistently missed deadlines despite top talent. Leaders introduced a simple ritual: daily "ownership declarations," where each team member stated one deliverable, they would own that day. Within six months, on-time delivery soared to 90%, and satisfaction scores climbed. The ritual didn't add more work – it made ownership visible, personal, and habitual.

Rituals are campfires. The spark is commitment, the wood is systems, and the flame is culture. Without regular feeding, the fire dies. With care, it spreads warmth across the organization.

Designing Rituals That Stick

Not every ritual endures. Some fade into hollow gestures. To design rituals that embed deeply, leaders should follow three principles:

1. **Simplicity** – Rituals must be easy to practice. One question, one declaration, one lesson is enough.
2. **Symbolism** – Rituals should carry deeper meaning. When leaders share their own failures, they signal that vulnerability is safe.
3. **Scalability** – Effective rituals work across contexts – in boardrooms or on shop floors.

A retail chain introduced a ritual called **"Customer Stories Monday."** Each week, teams shared a real customer experience, good or bad. Over time, the ritual reframed accountability beyond internal metrics to include the customer's voice. Engagement rose, and NPS scores improved. A simple ritual shifted focus and behavior.

Linking Loops and Rituals

Loops and rituals are not separate tools; they are complementary forces. Loops provide **structure**, ensuring accountability stays alive through constant correction. Rituals provide **meaning**, embedding accountability into the organization's identity. Together, they form a culture resilient to leadership changes, crises, and market shocks.

A global manufacturer demonstrated this power by combining structure and symbolism: weekly loops where commitments were reviewed every Friday, and recognition rituals where leaders celebrated acts of ownership. Over three years, productivity rose by 22%, safety incidents declined, and turnover fell. Loops fueled course correction. Rituals sustained the culture.

Together, loops and rituals form the drumbeat of accountability. Leaders set the rhythm, teams march to it, and culture carries it forward. When the drumbeat is steady, execution flows. When it falters, organizations stumble.

Turning Firefighting into Resilience

An airline plagued by recurring operational meltdowns had redesigned its accountability systems, yet slippage persisted. The breakthrough came when leadership layered in loops and rituals. Daily operational loops ensured every station reported commitments and outcomes, while a "Hero of the Day" ritual celebrated frontline ownership. Within a year, cancellations fell by 18%. The drumbeat of loops and rituals transformed firefighting into resilience.

Loops correct. Rituals embed. Together, they make accountability unshakable. Systems may change, leaders may come and go, and crises may strike – but when feedback loops and rituals are hardwired, ownership endures. This is the final layer of the **Accountability Action Framework™**. Next, we'll bring all eight sections together into a single message: accountability is not a program, a process, or a speech – it is the backbone of execution.

Accountability as the Backbone of Execution

Accountability is not glamorous. It doesn't make headlines or inspire applause. Yet without it, even the boldest strategies crumble. What we've explored in this chapter is simple but transformative: **accountability is the backbone of execution.**

Without a spine, the body cannot stand; without accountability, leadership cannot deliver.

Across these sections, we've seen accountability not as blame or bureaucracy but as **ownership** – the missing link between ambition and impact. We've learned how to surface gaps, climb from excuses to ownership, balance clarity with autonomy, and reinforce accountability through loops and rituals. Together, these practices form a system where execution becomes inevitable.

The Integrated Picture:

- Leaders make hidden gaps visible.
- Teams climb the ladder from denial to ownership.
- Systems balance top-down clarity with bottom-up autonomy.
- Feedback loops recycle commitments into learning.
- Rituals turn ownership into habit.

This is accountability not as theory but as practice. Not as punishment but as empowerment. Not as illusion but as reality.

Pause and Reflect

As you close this chapter, look at how ownership lives in your organization and ask yourself:

- Where does accountability blur or vanish in my organization?
- Do we name specific owners for critical outcomes, or do we hide behind collective responsibility?
- How do we respond when results fall short – with blame, excuses, or curiosity and learning?
- Where have we confused empowerment with leadership, granting autonomy without clarity or support?
- What would change if accountability became a shared cultural norm rather than a top-down demand?

These are not theoretical questions – they are mirrors. Accountability begins not with the organization but with the leader.

Next Step on the Journey

Accountability is the heartbeat of execution. It's the quiet, consistent pulse that turns plans into progress and intentions into impact. Without it, the best strategies remain ink on a page. With it, even modest ideas can transform entire organizations.

Think of a rowing team: without clear roles and shared rhythm, the boat spins in circles, no matter how strong the rowers are. Accountability sets the rhythm – aligning effort, clarifying direction, and creating the conditions for movement. As you step into the next chapter, remember that ownership isn't about blame – it's about belief. And once ownership is alive, the next task is to make sure that everyone understands the journey. That is the power of communication – not just speaking, but shaping shared understanding that drives collective action.

CHAPTER FOUR

Communication

The Power of Clarity in Leadership

"Clarity is not about saying more; it's about ensuring nothing gets lost when it matters most."

Beyond Speeches – Communicating for Impact

Most leaders think of communication as a performance: the big speech, the quarterly town hall, the carefully worded memo. But real leadership communication is not measured in applause after a speech; it is measured in clarity of action after the room is empty.

True communication is less about moments of inspiration and more about ecosystems of understanding. Teams don't disengage because their leaders failed to inspire them once. They disengage because day-to-day communication leaves them confused, overloaded, or in the dark.

The challenge for leaders is to move from **communication as performance** to **communication as execution.**

Information vs. Communication

One of the most common traps is confusing the **sharing of information** with the **act of communication.**

- **Information** is one-way: leaders push out facts, updates, and memos.
- **Communication** is two-way: leaders ensure messages are understood, absorbed, and acted upon.

In other words, if the message doesn't land, there has been no communication. An executive at a logistics company once admitted:
"We sent 14 emails about the new policy. Then we were shocked no one followed it."

What failed? Not the frequency of information, but the absence of communication. Leaders assumed volume equalled clarity. Instead, it created noise.

The Four-Part Framework for Impactful Communication

Great leadership communication consistently answers four questions in sequence.

1. **Context** – Why this matters now.
2. **Story** – The narrative that frames it in human terms.
3. **Data** – The facts, evidence, or proof points that anchor credibility.
4. **Call to Action** – What happens next, and who owns it.

This order matters. Story without data is empty rhetoric. Data without story is dry and forgettable. Context without a call-to-action breeds cynicism. The formula keeps communication both inspiring and actionable.

At one of the consumer goods companies, the CEO faced resistance to a digital transformation. Previous attempts failed because leaders drowned staff in slides of technical specifications. This time, the CEO reframed the approach:

- **Context**: "Our competitors are outpacing us digitally. If we don't catch up, we'll lose relevance."
- **Story**: He described a frontline worker struggling with outdated systems and customers frustrated with delays.
- **Data**: He shared performance gaps and industry benchmarks.
- **Call to Action**: Clear roles for teams in the rollout, with timelines and checkpoints.

The shift in approach sparked alignment. Within weeks, cross-functional teams were volunteering ideas instead of resisting.

From Corporate-Speak to Human-Speak

Another barrier to impact is the overuse of jargon, acronyms, and corporate-speak. These may feel efficient but often obscure meaning.

Consider these two statements:

- *"We need to leverage synergies to maximize operational efficiency."*
- *"We need teams to share resources so we can deliver faster and cheaper."*

The second is human-speak. People act on what they understand.

A CEO of a manufacturing company reduced jargon in all executive communications. Instructions were rewritten in plain English. Acronym-heavy decks were banned in all-hands meetings. The result was more than cosmetic – frontline workers reported a higher understanding of strategy, and engagement survey scores improved.

Leader's Discipline: Every message should pass the *"would a frontline employee understand this without context?"* test.

Storytelling as a Tool of Leadership

Stories are not entertainment; they are vehicles for meaning. The human brain processes stories up to 22 times more effectively than data alone. In leadership, stories do three things:

1. Make strategy relatable (from abstract to personal).
2. Anchor memory (people forget numbers but remember narratives).
3. Humanize leadership (building trust through vulnerability).

Leaders often underestimate how small, authentic stories can shift culture. Sharing a lesson from a personal mistake builds credibility. Sharing a frontline employee's success story reinforces desired behaviours more than any PowerPoint slide.

Leader Tip: Build a story bank – a set of 10–15 short, true stories aligned with your organization's values and strategy. Rotate them in communications to reinforce consistency.

Lighthouse vs. Lantern

Think of communication as light.

- A **lantern** lights up everything vaguely but without focus. It creates brightness, but people don't know where to walk.
- A **lighthouse** cuts through the dark with a clear, narrow beam, guiding ships safely to shore.

Leaders who communicate like lighthouses bring focus, direction, and safety. Those who communicate like lanterns spread activity without clarity.

Step-by-Step Guide for Leaders

1. **Audit your current style.** Review your last five messages. Were they clear, human, and actionable? Or vague, corporate, and forgettable?
2. **Apply the Context → Story → Data → Call to Action framework.** Draft messages using this order, not as afterthoughts.
3. **Ban jargon.** Challenge your team to translate strategy into human-speak.
4. **Use stories intentionally.** Keep them short, relatable, and authentic.
5. **Choose lighthouse over lantern.** Focus communication on what matters most, not everything that could be said.

Leadership communication is not about being the loudest voice in the room. It is about being the clearest. When leaders shift from speeches to ecosystems, from corporate-speak to human-speak, and from information to communication, they unlock execution.

The next dimension of this shift is transparency. If clarity builds understanding, transparency builds trust. And trust is the true currency of leadership communication.

The Art of Transparent Leadership

If clarity is the engine of execution, transparency is the fuel that keeps it running. People don't expect leaders to have all the answers. But they do expect leaders to be honest about what they know, what they don't, and how decisions are made.

Transparency is not about oversharing every detail. It is about building **trust through openness.** When trust is high, people move with speed and confidence. When trust is low, even simple changes stall under suspicion and second-guessing.

Transparency as Trust Currency

Every message leaders send is a deposit or withdrawal in the trust account. Withholding information, spinning bad news, or hiding behind vague promises erodes trust quickly.

Conversely, sharing context, admitting uncertainty, and explaining decisions – even unpopular ones – builds credibility. Employees can accept tough truths when they believe leaders are levelling with them.

In a manufacturing company, leadership faced a tough cost-cutting program. In the past, they softened language and avoided direct conversations. Employees filled the gaps with rumours, and morale tanked.

This time, the new plant director took a different approach. In the first town hall, he said:

- *"Here's what I know: we must reduce costs by 15% to stay competitive."*
- *"Here's what I don't know: which functions will be affected. We'll decide this in the next 60 days."*
- *"Here's what I promise: we'll communicate decisions within 24 hours of being made."*

The Candor did not remove anxiety, but it built trust. Employees later reported that while the cuts were painful, they felt respected – and engagement levels stabilized instead of collapsing.

The "I Know / I Don't Know / I'll Find Out" Tool

Leaders often fear admitting they don't have all the answers. Yet pretending otherwise damages credibility. A simple discipline:

- **I know** → Share facts you're certain about.
- **I don't know** → Acknowledge limits.
- **I'll find out** → Commit to follow-up and deliver.

This approach signals both competence and humility. Teams value honesty far more than false confidence.

Explaining the "Why" Behind Decisions

Transparency isn't only about facts – it's about rationale. When leaders explain the *why* behind decisions, they reduce resistance and increase alignment. Even if people disagree with the outcome, they understand the reasoning.

Example phrases leaders can use:

- *"We chose this option because..."*
- *"Here are the trade-offs we considered..."*
- *"Here's why we said no to the alternative..."*

Without this, employees often assume hidden agendas. With it, they see logic and fairness.

Normalizing Failure Through Transparency

In opaque cultures, mistakes are hidden, lessons are lost, and blame thrives. Transparent leaders flip the script: they surface failures, share what was learned, and encourage others to do the same.

A bus operator faced a major system outage during peak travel season. Instead of hiding the issue behind technical jargon, the COO held a press conference:

- Explained the system failure in plain terms.
- Shared the recovery timeline honestly.
- Took responsibility instead of blaming vendors.

While customers were frustrated, the candour minimized reputational damage. Employees reported pride that leadership "told the truth instead of spinning a story."

Practical Rituals That Reinforce Transparency

- **Decision Logs:** Summarize key decisions, rationale, and next steps; make them accessible to teams.
- **Open Q&A Forums:** Monthly sessions where employees can ask anything.
- **Failure Reviews:** Post-mortems framed as "What did we learn?" not "Who is at fault?"
- **Leader Diaries:** Weekly reflections from leaders on decisions, priorities, and lessons.

These rituals shift transparency from occasional moments to a cultural norm.

The Transparency Spectrum

Transparency is not binary; it exists on a spectrum:

1. **Opaque** – Decisions made behind closed doors, little context shared.
2. **Selective** – Leaders share only what feels safe.
3. **Open** – Leaders share facts and rationale consistently.
4. **Transparent Culture** – Teams expect openness and contribute to it.

Most organizations hover between selective and open. Moving toward transparency requires courage, but it pays exponential dividends in speed and trust.

The Clear Glass Window

Think of transparency like a window.

- An opaque window keeps people guessing. They imagine what's happening inside – often worse than reality.
- A clear window shows what's really happening. Even if the view isn't perfect, people trust what they see.

Leaders who communicate like clear glass windows reduce suspicion and build resilience.

Step-by-Step Guide for Leaders

1. **Audit your default style** → Do I over-protect information or over-spin messages?
2. **Adopt the "I Know / I Don't Know / I'll Find Out" tool** → Practice humility.
3. **Explain rationale** → Don't just state outcomes; share the trade-offs.
4. **Normalize failure** → Share lessons publicly.
5. **Install rituals** → Decision logs, open Q&As, failure reviews.

Transparent communication builds trust, but trust without discipline can still waste time. The next challenge for leaders is to shift from endless conversations to meaningful ones – turning meetings from a drain into a driver of execution.

From Excessive Meetings to Meaningful Conversations

Few things drain organizational energy more than poorly run meetings. Leaders call them to share information, align teams, or make decisions – yet most meetings achieve none of these goals. Instead, they become long, unfocused rituals of wasted time.

Surveys consistently show that managers spend up to **50–70% of their time in meetings**, and employees report that at least half of those meetings are unnecessary. The result is predictable: exhausted teams, delayed decisions, and "meeting walls" where people stop listening entirely.

The problem is not the meeting itself. The problem is the lack of discipline in how leaders design and run them.

The Meeting Wall Problem

In one of the pharmaceutical company, project managers complained that by Wednesday each week, their calendars were completely blocked. They called it the "meeting wall." Actual project execution happened after hours or on weekends.

When an internal audit was conducted, leaders realized:

- 60% of recurring meetings had no clear purpose.
- Fewer than 20% produced documented actions.

- Multiple teams met separately to discuss the same issue.

The conclusion was sobering: meetings were not accelerating execution – they were replacing it.

From Update Sessions to Value Conversations

The biggest culprit is the "update meeting." Teams spend hours sharing information that could have been sent in a three-paragraph summary or dashboard.

Rule of Thumb: If the purpose is only to inform, a meeting is unnecessary. If the purpose is to align, decide, or solve, a meeting may be justified.

Shifting from updates to conversations means asking three critical questions before calling a meeting:

1. **Why do we need to talk?**
2. **What outcome must this conversation produce?**
3. **What is the most efficient format to achieve it?**

The Red Thread of Meetings

Every meeting must have a **red thread** – a clear through-line that connects beginning to end. Leaders can use three filters:

- **Purpose** → What is the one thing this meeting must achieve?
- **Product** → What tangible output will be created (decision, plan, next steps)?
- **Process** → How will the group get there (discussion, voting, prioritization)?

Without a red thread, meetings meander. With it, they move.

Cutting 60% of Meetings

At a regional bank, employee engagement surveys revealed that "pointless meetings" were the top frustration. The executive team decided to run an experiment. They:

- Banned all recurring meetings for two weeks.
- Required every new meeting request to state purpose, outcome, and

agenda in 100 words or less.
- Allowed only 30- or 45-minute blocks (no default 60s).

The outcome:

- 60% fewer meetings held.
- Decision speed increased.
- Employees reported higher focus and energy.

After the pilot, leaders institutionalized the practice with "meeting charters" and quarterly audits.

The 70-20-10 Rule for Conversation Discipline

- **70% of meeting time** → Discussion, problem-solving, decision-making.
- **20% of meeting time** → Clarifying questions and updates.
- **10% of meeting time** → Confirming actions and owners.

Most organizations reverse this ratio – 70% updates, 20% unstructured debate, 10% rushed wrap-up. The result is noise, not execution.

Shifting the Medium: Beyond the Conference Room

Not all conversations belong in formal meetings. Leaders can replace them with lighter, faster formats:

- **Dashboards**: Real-time updates shared visually, reducing need for verbal reports.
- **Digital Channels**: Quick alignment via chat platforms.
- **Walk-and-Talks**: Informal 15-minute conversations that build connection and solve small issues.

A fast-scaling tech firm realized that meeting overload was slowing product cycles. Leadership replaced weekly progress reviews with a live dashboard accessible to all teams. Leaders held biweekly walk-and-talks instead of formal updates. Within three months, time-to-market improved by 20%.

Orchestra vs. Noise

Meetings are like orchestras. When well-designed, each instrument contributes, the conductor provides direction, and the result is harmony. But without structure, they devolve into noise – lots of sound, little music.

Leaders who design conversations like orchestras ensure every voice has its place and timing. Those who don't subject their teams to endless rehearsals without ever performing.

Step-by-Step Guide for Leaders

1. **Audit current meetings:** Which produce outcomes? Which don't?
2. **Kill or redesign:** Cancel update-only sessions. Redesign others with a clear red thread.
3. **Adopt the 70-20-10 rule:** Protect time for decisions, not updates.
4. **Experiment with alternatives:** Dashboards, digital channels, walk-and-talks.
5. **Institutionalize charters:** Require every meeting to state purpose, outcome, and agenda in advance.

When leaders shift from excessive meetings to meaningful conversations, they return time, energy, and clarity to their teams. But conversation alone is not enough. Execution also depends on how quickly decisions can be made and acted upon. That's where **real-time decision-making** comes in.

The Power of Real-Time Decision-Making

Clarity and transparency build trust. Meaningful conversations reduce waste. But leadership still fails without one more ingredient: **speed.**

In today's environment, the cost of slow decision-making is steep. Opportunities vanish, competitors outpace, and teams grow frustrated waiting for approvals. A study of Fortune 500 executives once found that **decision latency – the time it takes to make and communicate a decision – was one of the top three barriers to execution.**

Leaders who communicate effectively understand that decision-making is not just a process. It is a communication act. Decisions that are clear, timely, and well-communicated unleash momentum. Decisions that are slow or muddled breed paralysis.

Decision-Making as Communication

Many organizations treat decision-making as a hidden process: a small group debates privately, announces results late, and shares little about how the conclusion was reached. The result is confusion and resistance.

But decisions are themselves **moments of communication.** They signal priorities, values, and direction. The way a decision is made and shared communicates as much as the content itself.

Hospital Huddles

A large hospital system struggled with patient throughput in emergency care. Delays were constant because doctors, nurses, and administrators escalated decisions through multiple approval layers.

A new leader introduced **real-time decision huddles**:

- Multidisciplinary teams gathered every morning for 15 minutes.
- Critical issues (bed shortages, staffing, urgent transfers) were surfaced.
- Decisions were made on the spot, recorded, and communicated immediately.

The impact was dramatic. Average patient wait times dropped by 30%. Staff reported higher confidence because they could see alignment in action. The secret was not just better processes – it was visible, real-time decision communication.

The 70% Rule

Waiting for perfect information is one of the biggest killers of speed. General Colin Powell famously applied the "70% rule": make a decision when you have roughly 70% of the information you'd like.

- At less than 70% → you're guessing.
- At more than 70% → you're delaying.

Leaders who wait for certainty lose momentum. Leaders who act with 70% clarity move, learn, and adjust.

RACI for Role Clarity

Speed also depends on role clarity. When no one knows who owns the decision, issues linger in limbo.

RACI Model:

- **Responsible** → Who executes the task.
- **Accountable** → Who makes the final call.
- **Consulted** → Who provides input.
- **Informed** → Who must be updated.

Applying RACI to decisions prevents duplication and clarifies communication.

Leader Tip: Every major project decision should have one named accountable person – not a committee.

Retailer Accelerating Time-to-Market

A local retailer noticed its product launches were lagging behind competitors. Postmortems showed decisions about packaging, pricing, and promotions were delayed in cross-functional approvals.

Leaders implemented three changes:

1. **Decision Huddles** → Small cross-functional groups with authority to decide in real time.
2. **RACI Maps** → Clear ownership for each stage.
3. **70% Rule** → Teams empowered to move forward without waiting for certainty.

Result: time-to-market improved by six weeks, sales rose, and employee frustration dropped.

The Pit Crew

Think of real-time decision-making like a Formula 1 pit crew. In 2–3 seconds, dozens of small actions happen flawlessly: wheels change, adjustments are made, and the car is back on track.

The crew does not debate endlessly or escalate approvals mid-race. They are aligned, practiced, and empowered to act. In the same way, organizations with fast, transparent decision-making keep their engines running while others stall in the pits.

Step-by-Step Guide for Leaders

1. **Audit your decision latency** → How long does it take from issue raised → decision made → decision communicated?
2. **Introduce decision huddles** → Short, frequent forums with authority to decide.
3. **Apply the 70% rule** → Stop waiting for perfection; move and adapt.
4. **Map RACI roles** → Ensure every decision has one clear owner.
5. **Communicate decisions visibly** → Document rationale, next steps, and timelines immediately.

Real-time decision-making transforms communication from a bottleneck into a catalyst. But even when speed is achieved, another barrier often lingers: bureaucracy. Messages still get stuck in layers of approvals, and clarity gets lost in translation. To truly accelerate execution, leaders must tackle bureaucracy head-on.

Eliminating Bureaucracy in Leadership Communication

Clarity. Transparency. Speed. All of these collapse if messages are buried under bureaucracy. Many organizations have mastered creating noise without meaning – multiple approvals, endless CCs, reports that travel up five levels before reaching the people who actually need the information.

Bureaucracy slows execution not because people lack intelligence, but because communication gets tangled in a web of hierarchy. The tragedy is that by the time a decision or message reaches the frontline, it is often diluted, delayed, or distorted.

The Communication "Telephone Game"

Anyone who played the "telephone game" as a child knows how messages degrade as they pass through multiple people. The same happens in organizations.

A fintech company discovered that product launch delays were not due to technical hurdles, but communication bottlenecks. Every marketing decision needed six layers of sign-off. By the time approval came, customer needs had shifted, and competitors had already moved.

Leaders diagnosed the issue as bureaucracy, not execution. They restructured approvals so cross-functional "decision squads" could act autonomously within guidelines. Time-to-market improved, and employee frustration dropped dramatically.

Why Bureaucracy Thrives

1. **Fear of Mistakes** → Leaders add more approvals to avoid blame.
2. **Status Preservation** → Managers hold onto information to appear important.
3. **Legacy Habits** → Layers remain because "we've always done it this way."

Bureaucracy survives on mistrust. Breaking it requires leaders to replace mistrust with trust, and opacity with clarity.

The Communication Charter

A **communication charter** is a set of agreed rules that streamline how information flows. It ensures the right people get the right information at the right time – without unnecessary noise.

Elements of a charter:

- **Direct-to-Frontline Principle** → Leaders communicate directly to those executing, not just managers.
- **Clarity of Ownership** → Each communication names who owns the message and next steps.
- **No Endless CCs** → Limit distribution lists to those who must act, not everyone who might be interested.
- **Fast Channels First** → Urgent decisions through live discussions, not email chains.

When institutionalized, a communication charter creates alignment and prevents bureaucracy from creeping back.

Bank Flattening Layers

At a regional bank, risk updates had to travel through three regional committees before reaching branch managers. By the time information arrived, the situation had changed.

The COO implemented a new system:

- Updates bypassed committees and went directly to branches via digital dashboards.
- Committees shifted focus from approving every message to auditing accuracy quarterly.
- Branch managers received near real-time updates, improving compliance and customer outcomes.

This flattening of layers not only accelerated communication but also restored accountability to those closest to execution.

Practical Tools for Cutting Bureaucracy

- **Skip-Level Conversations** → Leaders talk directly to teams two or three layers down.
- **Single-Point Approvals** → Assign one accountable decision-maker, not committees.
- **Open Dashboards** → Replace cascaded reports with live, transparent data.
- **Escalation Lanes** → Define when issues must go upward, preventing unnecessary bottlenecks.

Leader Tip: Ask in every meeting — *"Is this decision waiting on more approvals than it needs?"*

Bureaucracy is like a trail blocked by debris. People spend more energy climbing over obstacles than reaching the destination. Leaders who clear the path remove unnecessary hurdles, allowing energy to flow where it matters most: execution.

Step-by-Step Guide for Leaders

1. **Map your current approval chains.** How many steps does each message or decision take?
2. **Identify redundant layers.** Ask: Who adds real value vs. who just passes information?

3. **Design a communication charter.** Set principles for speed, clarity, and ownership.
4. **Pilot direct-to-frontline communication.** Share updates directly with execution teams.
5. **Institutionalize dashboards and skip-levels.** Make transparency structural, not ad hoc.

By stripping bureaucracy out of communication, leaders transform organizations from slow, cautious, and mistrustful into fast, confident, and aligned. And when clarity, transparency, meaningful conversations, real-time decision-making, and bureaucracy-free communication converge, communication becomes what it was always meant to be: the ultimate execution multiplier.

The Leadership Imperative

The message of this chapter is simple but demanding: **leaders are not just speakers; they are Chief Clarity Officers.** Every message you deliver is either fuel or friction. Every delay, layer, or vague phrase is a tax on execution.

Great leaders understand that communication is not an event. It is a system. A system where:

- Clarity replaces noise.
- Transparency replaces suspicion.
- Conversations replace monologues.
- Decisions replace delays.
- Trust replaces bureaucracy.

The Execution Signal

Imagine a radio signal. When static drowns out the frequency, listeners tune out. But when the signal is strong and clear, it cuts through distance, noise, and distraction.

Communication is that signal. When leaders broadcast with clarity, people align, act, and execute. When they don't, even the most talented teams stumble in confusion.

The choice is stark: drown your organization in static, or become the strong signal that cuts through. Leaders who choose clarity choose execution. Leaders who choose execution choose impact.

Pause and Reflect

As you close this chapter, look at where messages land—or don't—and ask yourself:

- How often does information flow in my organization without true understanding following it?
- Where have messages been sent but never truly landed – and what were the consequences?
- Do I encourage dialogue, or do I mistake one-way updates for communication?
- Where is complexity clouding clarity – and how can I translate strategy into plain language that sticks?
- What stories, metaphors, or rituals could I use to make meaning travel deeper and farther?

Next Step on the Journey

Communication is not the art of speaking – it's the science of being understood. It's what transforms plans from documents into shared purpose and turns individual efforts into collective momentum. Without it, even the most brilliant strategies drift in confusion; with it, they become movements.

Think of a conductor before an orchestra. Each musician may be world-class, but without shared rhythm and cues, the music dissolves into noise. Communication is that rhythm – the invisible alignment that turns effort into harmony. As you move forward, remember that leadership is not measured by the number of words you speak, but by the clarity of action that follows them. And once clarity has taken root, the next step is to fuel it – because execution isn't sustained by communication alone. It thrives on energy, ownership, and human connection. That's the power of **engagement**.

CHAPTER FIVE

Engagement

The Secret to High-Performance Teams

"People don't resist change itself; they resist the feeling of being unseen in the process of change."

The Psychology of Engagement

Why do some teams thrive in the face of challenge while others retreat into silence, cynicism, or apathy? The difference rarely lies in talent alone. Instead, it lies in how human brains and hearts respond to the environments they inhabit. Engagement, at its core, is not a perk or an optional cultural add-on. It is a biological, emotional, and structural foundation for productivity and innovation.

The Brain at Work: Chemistry of Connection and Withdrawal

Neuroscience offers a powerful lens for leaders. When people feel safe, valued, and connected, their brains release **dopamine** and **oxytocin**. These chemicals heighten motivation, build trust, and make collaboration natural. Teams in this state are energized, willing to experiment, and resilient to stress.

But the opposite is just as true. When people feel excluded, dismissed, or threatened, the brain triggers the amygdala's **fight-or-flight response**. Energy shifts from creativity to self-protection. Withdrawal, resistance, and even subtle sabotage can follow. What looks like disengagement on the surface is often simply biology in defence mode.

Engagement, therefore, isn't a "nice-to-have." It is a survival response that either fuels growth or quietly starves it.

Disengagement ≠ Laziness

One of the most dangerous myths in leadership is the assumption that disengaged employees simply don't care. In truth, disengagement is rarely about laziness; it is about unmet emotional needs at work.

Consider three silent killers of engagement:

- **Fear**: "If I speak up, I'll be punished."
- **Confusion**: "I don't understand where we're going or why."
- **Disconnection**: "No one notices what I contribute."

Gallup research confirms the scale of this issue: nearly **85% of employees worldwide** are not engaged or actively disengaged – not because they lack motivation, but because the conditions around them block motivation from surfacing.

Leadership Myth vs. Reality of Disengagement

Myth	Reality
People disengage because they are lazy	People disengage because fear, confusion, or disconnection overwhelms them
More pressure will spark motivation	More pressure without support deepens resistance
Engagement is about perks and rewards	Engagement is about safety, meaning, and connection

The Reframe for Leaders

When leaders interpret silence, apathy, or resistance as laziness, they misdiagnose the problem. The true question isn't "Why aren't they working harder?" but "What conditions are keeping them from showing up fully?"

The psychology of engagement begins here: treating human behaviour at work not as a mystery, but as a predictable response to whether people feel seen, supported, and connected.

Why People Resist Change

Leaders often misinterpret resistance to change as defiance, laziness, or stubbornness. In reality, resistance is rarely about rejecting the change itself. More often, it is about the **emotional toll of uncertainty, loss of control, or fear of failure.** Even the most talented, committed employees can hesitate or push back when their psychological needs feel threatened.

To understand resistance, we must look beneath the surface behaviours and trace the underlying forces that trigger disengagement.

Loss of Control: The Autonomy Threat

Change often feels like being pushed into a fast current without a paddle. Decisions are made about people, not with them. The psychological effect is profound because humans are wired for autonomy – the need to feel we have some say in how our lives unfold.

When autonomy is stripped away, resistance rises. It's not necessarily opposition to the **change itself**, but to the feeling of being powerless in the process. People are more likely to lean in when they are given a voice, however small, in shaping the path forward.

Lack of Clarity: The Anxiety of Uncertainty

The human brain craves certainty. It uses patterns and predictability to reduce anxiety and conserve energy. When change is introduced without clear reasoning or direction, the brain interprets this as danger.

Unclear communication breeds:

- **Anxiety** – people worry about hidden consequences.
- **Rumours** – in the absence of facts, speculation fills the gap.
- **Analysis paralysis** – hesitation replaces action.

In short, where there is ambiguity, engagement shuts down. A leader's role is to reduce uncertainty by repeatedly clarifying **the why, the what, and the how.**

Fear of Failure: The Silent Barrier

Change brings new systems, new expectations, and sometimes new roles. Beneath the surface, many employees wrestle with unspoken fears:

- *"What if I can't keep up?"*
- *"What if I'm exposed as not good enough?"*
- *"What if failure costs me my job?"*

This fear doesn't inspire risk-taking; it fuels self-protection. People retreat into familiar habits, avoid visibility, or resist new responsibilities. Leaders who dismiss fear as weakness miss the point. Fear is not weakness – it is the brain's natural defence mechanism against perceived threat.

The Leader's Reframe: Resistance as Data

What if resistance wasn't a problem to crush, but a signal to interpret? Each form of resistance points to an unmet need:

- Loss of control → need for **autonomy.**
- Lack of clarity → need for **certainty.**
- Fear of failure → need for **psychological safety.**

Seen this way, resistance becomes data for leaders – a mirror reflecting where communication, inclusion, or support is falling short. Instead of labelling people as resistant, effective leaders ask: *What need is not being met?*

Resistance is not a wall blocking progress. It is a signal flare, highlighting where engagement is most at risk. Leaders who recognize this shift from pushing change onto people to **inviting people into change.** And that is the foundation on which true engagement is built.

The Emotional Needs That Drive Engagement

Engagement doesn't begin with perks or pay checks. It begins with addressing the **emotional foundation** of human behaviour at work. People bring their whole selves into the workplace – their hopes, anxieties, and need for connection. If those needs are neglected, no amount of strategy or structure will spark genuine commitment.

Research and practice consistently reveal three universal drivers that determine how people show up: **Purpose, Belonging, and Progress.** These needs transcend industries and cultures. They are not "extras" for enlightened organizations; they are the oxygen that sustains performance.

Purpose: The Need for Meaning

At the core, people want to know that their work matters. Purpose answers questions like:

- *Why does this task exist?*
- *How does my effort connect to something bigger?*

Without purpose, work feels transactional. People do the minimum, waiting for the next pay check. With purpose, effort transforms into contribution. Leaders who make the connection between everyday tasks and broader outcomes light a spark that no incentive can match.

Purpose does not always mean grand missions or lofty visions. It can be as simple as linking a back-office analyst's report to the decisions that keep products safe, or reminding a frontline worker how their role protects customer trust.

In practice: Purpose gives meaning to effort. It transforms output into impact.

Belonging: The Need to Be Seen and Valued

Humans are wired for connection. Neuroscience shows that being excluded activates the same brain regions as physical pain. Belonging, therefore, is not a luxury – it is a survival instinct.

Belonging answers questions like:

- *Am I seen?*
- *Am I heard?*
- *Am I valued here?*

When belonging is absent, teams fragment into isolated individuals. Trust evaporates, voices go silent, and collaboration suffers. But when belonging is strong, individuals don't just contribute skills – they contribute energy, creativity, and loyalty.

For leaders, belonging is cultivated in moments: inviting input, recognizing effort, showing empathy, remembering a personal detail. Small signals of value accumulate into deep reservoirs of trust.

In practice: Belonging turns teams from collections of individuals into communities.

Progress: The Need for Growth and Momentum

Humans thrive on movement. Progress is the sense that effort today creates a better tomorrow. Without it, people stagnate, lose hope, or disengage.

Progress answers questions like:

- *Am I improving?*
- *Are we moving forward as a team?*
- *Is my contribution recognized?*

When leaders track milestones, celebrate small wins, and provide opportunities for growth, they feed progress. The psychological effect is powerful: momentum builds pride, pride builds motivation, and motivation sustains performance.

Progress is not only about promotions or big breakthroughs. It can be the visible completion of a project, mastering a skill, or being acknowledged for a job well done.

In practice: Progress fuels optimism, confidence, and pride.

Journey from Disengagement to Impact

Sarah was a frontline supervisor at a manufacturing plant when her company announced a major shift to automation. Overnight, her world was turned upside down. Half her team's tasks changed. She was handed new reporting tools with no training. Leadership stopped visiting the floor, relying instead on memos.

At first, Sarah tried to keep morale alive. She encouraged her team, offered suggestions, and kept working hard. But over time, discouragement set in. She stopped sharing ideas. Her voice in meetings grew flat. Quietly, she began searching for another job.

Her disengagement wasn't laziness – it was fear, confusion, and disconnection.

Then a new plant manager, Daniel, arrived. He did not push more memos or impose rigid directives. Instead, he:

- Walked the floor every morning.
- Asked, *"What's working? What's breaking? What do you need from me?"*
- Set up weekly check-ins where Sarah could voice concerns.
- Celebrated small wins publicly, from efficiency gains to safety milestones.

Within months, Sarah re-engaged. She proposed improvements to the automation rollout. She mentored younger supervisors. She became a go-to problem solver.

What made the difference?

- **Purpose**: She finally understood the *why* behind the shift.
- **Belonging**: She felt heard and valued.
- **Progress**: She saw her contributions shaping outcomes.

Sarah's story illustrates that when leaders meet the emotional needs of their people, disengagement transforms into ownership.

Purpose, belonging, and progress are not abstract ideals. They are practical levers leaders can activate every day. The challenge – and opportunity – lies in recognizing them as the invisible drivers behind visible performance. Addressing them is not optional. It is the essence of leadership in times of change.

Winning Over Resistance – The Leader's Role

If resistance is rooted in unmet needs, then the leader's role is not to push harder but to **create conditions where people choose engagement.** Change becomes sustainable not when leaders issue commands but when they build trust, invite participation, and honour the emotions that surface along the way.

Acknowledging Losses Honestly

Every change involves loss: familiar routines, old ways of working, sometimes even status or identity. Leaders who gloss over these losses send a subtle message – *your experience doesn't matter.*

Acknowledging loss is not a sign of weakness. It is a sign of respect. It tells people, *I see what this costs you, and I'm not minimizing it.* Leaders who openly recognize the sacrifices people make pave the way for acceptance and resilience.

Giving People a Voice in Shaping the Path

Humans resist being acted upon but embrace being invited to act. Even small opportunities for choice restore a sense of control.

This doesn't mean running organizations by committee or outsourcing tough calls. It means creating space for input:

- Inviting employees into pilot groups.
- Asking frontline teams to test new processes.
- Allowing staff to shape how a change is implemented, even if the *what* is non-negotiable.

When people feel their fingerprints on the process, resistance turns into ownership.

Offering Clear Direction and Removing Ambiguity

Confusion is the enemy of engagement. In moments of uncertainty, rumours grow faster than trust. Leaders must step into this void with clarity.

Clear direction does three things:

1. Anchors people in the *why* – why the change matters, why it cannot be ignored.
2. Provides visibility into the *what* – the outcomes and priorities to focus on.
3. Breaks down the *how* – the next few steps that reduce anxiety and create momentum.

Clarity does not eliminate resistance overnight, but it transforms fear into something people can work with.

Recognizing Effort, Not Just Results

During change, results often lag. If recognition is withheld until the finish line, people lose energy along the way. Leaders who acknowledge effort – the late-night troubleshooting, the willingness to speak up, the courage to try something new – fuel persistence.

Recognition of effort sends a deeper message: *you matter not just for what you deliver but for how you show up.* That message builds loyalty long after the project ends.

The Garden and the Gardener

Imagine an organization as a garden. If plants aren't thriving, a poor gardener blames the plants: *"They're weak. They're lazy."*

A wise gardener looks deeper: *"Is the soil right? Are they getting enough light? Do they have room to grow?"*

Leaders are gardeners. Engagement is not forced; it is cultivated. In the right conditions, even struggling plants can flourish. In the wrong conditions, even the most resilient will wither.

When leaders honour loss, give voice, bring clarity, and celebrate effort, they transform resistance into energy. The next step is to translate these behaviours into a framework – one that makes engagement less mystical and more practical. That framework is the **Engagement Formula.**

The Engagement Formula – Building a High-Trust Culture

Engagement is often described as elusive, even mysterious. Some teams "magically" have it, while others can't seem to spark it no matter how many programs or perks they introduce. But engagement is not magic. It is the product of deliberate conditions leaders can create.

Decades of research and field experience reveal a simple but powerful truth: when four ingredients come together, people move from compliance to commitment, from busywork to meaningful work, and from burnout to sustainable energy.

The formula is this:

Clarity + Autonomy + Recognition + Progress = High Engagement

This is not a slogan. It is a repeatable framework leaders can apply to any team, in any industry, at any stage of change. Let's break it down step by step.

Clarity → Clear Goals and Purpose

Why it matters
People cannot engage with what they do not understand. Without clarity, employees flounder, second-guess priorities, and fill the gaps with speculation.

Dimensions of Clarity

- **Strategic clarity**: Where is the organization going?
- **Operational clarity**: What do we expect of this team?
- **Personal clarity**: What does success look like in *my* role?

A Harvard Business Review study found that only **50% of employees clearly understand what is expected of them at work**. That means half of the workforce is operating in uncertainty – a direct killer of engagement.

In practice

- Anchor messages to the "why," not just the "what."
- Provide transparent priorities, even if they shift.
- Translate big goals into personal relevance.

Without clarity, energy leaks into confusion. With clarity, energy channels into progress.

Autonomy → Freedom to Own Work

Why it matters

Micromanagement suffocates creativity. Humans have a deep need for autonomy – the ability to shape how work is done. When leaders over-direct or second-guess, initiative dries up and frustration builds.

Autonomy in Action

- Trusting people to choose how to achieve outcomes.
- Giving room for experimentation and innovation.
- Encouraging constructive challenge to improve processes.

Leadership Reframe

Autonomy is not the absence of accountability. It is the presence of trust. True ownership emerges when people are free to make choices *and* are held responsible for results.

Micromanagement creates compliance. Autonomy creates commitment.

Recognition → Feeling Seen and Valued

Why it matters

Engaged people feel noticed. Recognition is one of the most powerful psychological drivers of human behaviour. When leaders recognize contributions – not just results but effort, progress, and courage – they reinforce the very behaviours they want repeated.

What Recognition Looks Like

- Specific, not generic: *"Your insight clarified the client's hesitation"* instead of *"Good job."*
- Timely, not delayed: immediate acknowledgment builds momentum.
- Multi-directional, not only top-down: peer-to-peer recognition strengthens community.

Impact
Gallup studies show that employees who receive regular recognition:

- Are more productive.
- Show higher loyalty.
- Report stronger well-being.

Recognition is not a perk. It is oxygen for engagement.

Progress → Momentum and Growth

Why it matters
Few things drain energy faster than the feeling of standing still. Humans are wired to crave progress. Whether it's mastering a skill, reaching a milestone, or contributing to a bigger win, visible improvement fuels hope and confidence.

Progress in Action

- Set clear milestones and make them visible.
- Celebrate small wins, not just big ones.
- Offer stretch opportunities and learning pathways.

Psychological Effect
Progress builds pride. Pride builds motivation. Motivation sustains performance. It is the compounding effect that keeps teams resilient.

People don't disengage because the goal is hard. They disengage because they can't see movement.

Practical Tools and Rituals for Leaders

Bringing the formula to life requires more than awareness; it requires intentional rituals. Leaders can weave these into their weekly rhythm:

Engagement Check-Ins

- Weekly or biweekly one-on-ones.
- Three core questions: *What's going well? Where are you stuck? What support do you need?*
- Focus on listening, not directing.

Shared Wins Celebrations

- Rituals that spotlight progress and achievement.
- Examples: "Win of the Week" shout-outs, digital kudos boards, short leader emails.
- Impact: builds pride, reinforces values, amplifies momentum.

Simple Feedback Loops

- Replace annual reviews with real-time feedback.
- Spontaneous coaching moments or peer-to-peer circles.
- Specific, behaviour-based feedback builds trust and growth.

The Engagement Effect

Maria, a mid-level manager at a consumer goods company, led a team that had been struggling: missed deadlines, low energy in meetings, and high turnover.

After a leadership workshop, Maria decided to experiment with the Engagement Formula. She:

- Clarified goals in plain, jargon-free language.
- Stepped back from micromanaging and trusted her team to own projects.
- Began every meeting with recognition of progress, however small.
- Tracked milestones publicly, so movement was visible.

Within three months, productivity improved, engagement survey scores rose, and the team's mood shifted from resignation to optimism. Maria's reflection was telling:

"Engagement isn't about pushing people harder. It's about creating the conditions where they want to give their best."

The Energy Grid

Think of engagement as an energy grid that lights up an organization.

- **Clarity** is the wiring – it connects people to purpose.
- **Autonomy** is the voltage – it powers ownership.

- **Recognition** is the light – it makes people feel seen.
- **Progress** is the current – it keeps momentum flowing.

When all four flow together, teams illuminate possibility. Without them, the system flickers, stalls, or goes dark.

The Engagement Formula shows that high trust and high energy are not accidental. They are built deliberately, through clarity, autonomy, recognition, and progress. Yet one element in particular – recognition – deserves deeper exploration, because it is the amplifier of all the others.

Recognition-Driven Engagement – How to Motivate Without Micromanaging

For decades, leaders assumed a simple equation: more perks + more pressure = more motivation. Companies responded with flashier bonuses, stricter targets, and an endless stream of perks. But motivation built on perks fades quickly, and motivation built on pressure burns out even faster.

The truth is clear: **neither perks nor pressure build sustainable engagement.** What sustains performance is something far more human – the feeling of being seen, valued, and appreciated. Recognition is not soft. It is one of the hardest drivers of loyalty, performance, and well-being.

The Myth of Motivation: Perks and Pressure

Perks excite, but briefly. A new office perk – free lunches, gym memberships, ping-pong tables – creates novelty but loses its shine within weeks.

Pressure pushes, but harshly. Aggressive quotas, tighter deadlines, or public rankings may spike performance in the short term, but they also fuel resentment, stress, and turnover.

Studies by Gallup and Harvard Business Review confirm this:

- **Extrinsic motivators** like pay and perks create short-lived effects.
- **Excessive pressure** leads to burnout and disengagement.

The sustainable motivator? **Recognition – the simple act of being noticed and appreciated.**

The Power of Recognition

Recognition isn't optional or ornamental. It is oxygen. When people feel noticed, they lean in; when they feel invisible, they check out. Recognition strengthens trust, reinforces desired behaviours, and builds pride.

Three qualities make recognition powerful:

1. **Specific Praise**
   Generic praise – "Good job" – fades fast. Specific praise sticks because it shows attention and intention. Saying "Your analysis spotted a trend we were missing," or "The way you calmed that client shifted the entire meeting," makes people feel truly seen. Specificity not only validates the individual but also reinforces the behaviours leaders want repeated.

2. **Timely Acknowledgment**
   Praise delayed is impact diluted. A compliment about something that happened months ago feels disconnected. Recognition given in the moment sparks immediate positive emotion and strengthens the link between action and reward.

3. **Peer-to-Peer Shoutouts**
   Recognition should not be the leader's monopoly. When peers call out each other's contributions, trust deepens and hierarchy flattens. A simple kudos board, shoutout round at the start of meetings, or digital recognition channel turns recognition into a shared cultural rhythm.

Tools to Build a Recognition Culture

Recognition thrives when it shifts from occasional gestures to consistent rituals. Leaders can design simple, repeatable practices that make recognition part of everyday culture.

1. Recognition Rituals

- Weekly wins meetings where each person shares one proud moment.
- Leader shoutouts at the start of meetings.
- Friday appreciation emails spotlighting contributions.

Tip: Keep it public, brief, and authentic.

2. Digital Platforms for Public Praise

- Slack or Teams kudos channels.
- Peer-nomination platforms.
- Recognition walls on dashboards.

Why it works: It normalizes appreciation, creates visibility, and builds positive feedback loops.

3. Small but Meaningful Rewards
Recognition doesn't have to be financial.

- Handwritten thank-you notes.
- Personalized tokens of appreciation.
- Flex hours or time off.

Tip: Match the gesture to the person. The most powerful recognition is personal, not transactional.

Marcus's Team Turnaround

Marcus led a product design team in a fast-paced startup. When deadlines slipped and morale dropped, he believed the solution was more pressure. He imposed stricter deadlines, added approval layers, and worked late expecting the same from his team.

The result? Two resignations and a silent, disengaged team.

After attending a leadership retreat, Marcus changed course. He:

- Shifted from control to trust, giving designers more autonomy.
- Launched a weekly recognition ritual, celebrating wins every Friday.
- Practiced spontaneous, real-time praise in meetings and on Slack.

Six months later, deadlines were hit, ideas flowed, and engagement scores soared. Marcus's reflection was telling:

"When people feel seen, they step up. When they feel squeezed, they shut down."

Recognition as Oxygen

Picture a campfire.

- **Autonomy** is the fuel.
- **Clarity** is the spark.
- **Progress** is the flame.
  But recognition? Recognition is the oxygen.

Without oxygen, the flame suffocates. With it, the fire roars to life, warming and illuminating everyone around it.

Recognition powers belonging and pride, but it does more. It links directly to accountability. When people feel trusted and valued, they don't just work harder – they take greater ownership. That is where engagement and accountability begin to reinforce each other.

Engagement and Accountability – Complementary Forces

Many leaders fall into a dangerous trap: believing they must choose between driving results and building connection. In their minds, it's a trade-off – either you focus on performance or you focus on people. Either you hold feet to the fire or you inspire hearts and minds.

This is a false choice. Engagement and accountability are not opposites; they are amplifiers of each other. When people feel trusted and valued, they care more. When they care more, they own outcomes. When they own outcomes, accountability rises – not because it is demanded, but because it is chosen.

The relationship is circular, self-reinforcing, and powerful:

Engagement → Ownership → Accountability → Deeper Engagement → Stronger Accountability → High Performance.

The Virtuous Loop: Step by Step

1. People Who Feel Valued → Engage More
When leaders recognize contributions, include people in decisions, and trust their judgment, intrinsic motivation is activated. People bring not just compliance but commitment.

2. Engaged People → Own Outcomes
Engagement is not only emotional; it is behavioural. Engaged employees go beyond what is asked. They bring ideas, challenge assumptions, and shift from *"my job"* to *"our mission."*

3. Ownership → Increases Accountability
Ownership is the heartbeat of accountability. People who feel like owners keep promises, admit mistakes, and push for excellence. People who feel like cogs do the opposite – waiting for instructions, blaming others, or doing the bare minimum.

Leadership Reframe
You don't get real accountability by demanding it. You get it by cultivating conditions where people choose it.

What Happens When One Is Missing?

Accountability Without Engagement = Compliance and Resentment
Picture a sales team measured by daily reports, strict quotas, and leaderboard rankings. Results rise briefly, but creativity collapses, trust erodes, and star performers leave. Compliance delivers numbers but breeds brittleness.

Engagement Without Accountability = Chaos and Drift
Now imagine a startup with flexible hours, casual culture, and plenty of enthusiasm – but projects run late, quality slips, and no one owns outcomes. Without accountability, engagement becomes noise without music.

Engagement + Accountability = Sustainable High Performance
The sweet spot is not compromise but integration. Think of a high-performing sports team: demanding standards matched with deep investment, feedback flowing in all directions, teammates holding each other accountable. That's the model for any resilient organization.

In one fast-growing tech company, a troubling split had emerged: sales were hitting targets, but customer renewals were falling. Product teams were shipping updates regularly, but not in sync with actual client needs. The leadership team recognized the gap and acted decisively. Sales bonuses were restructured to reward long-term customer success rather than just deals closed. Product evaluations began to include cross-team collaboration scores. Monthly "customer experience" town halls were introduced to share wins and lessons across departments. Peer-nominated awards celebrated collaborative achievements over individual heroics. As trust deepened across silos, both engagement and accountability rose – and so did customer retention.

At a manufacturing plant plagued by chronic delays, the culture had soured. Leaders demanded explanations, managers passed blame, and frontline workers disengaged in silence. When a new director, Raj, stepped in, he focused less on control and more on connection. Daily "what's working, what's stuck" huddles gave everyone a voice. Problems were addressed collectively rather than assigned as blame. Wins were reframed to celebrate team collaboration, not just standout individuals. Mistakes triggered learning reviews instead of punishment. Within months, delays dropped by 25%, turnover fell, and trust across layers of the organization began to rebuild. Raj later reflected, *"When people feel safe and responsible, they stop hiding – and they start leading."*

The Leadership Behaviours That Make It Work

1. **Model Accountability with Humility**
   Say, *"Here's what I could have done better."* Show you own mistakes and learn publicly.
2. **Set Clear, Meaningful Expectations**
   Define success, explain why it matters, and involve the team in shaping goals.
3. **Provide Ongoing Feedback**
   Don't wait for annual reviews. Offer quick, clear course corrections and appreciation in real time.
4. **Balance High Standards with High Support**
   Push people to stretch but provide resources, coaching, and encouragement.
5. **Celebrate Shared Wins**
   Name both the *what* and the *how* – recognizing effort and collaboration, not just results.

Pitfalls vs Fixes

Pitfall	Fix
Using accountability as punishment	Frame it as commitment, not control
Confusing busyness with ownership	Focus on outcomes, not activity
Relying only on top-down accountability	Build peer accountability and self-management
Ignoring the emotional climate	Ensure safety and support are present

Practical Tools to Build the Engagement–Accountability Bridge

- **Accountability Agreements**: Define commitments together.
  "We agree to review progress every Friday."
- **Shared Scorecards**: Make progress visible to everyone, not just leaders.
- **Peer Recognition Programs**: Teammates highlight accountability wins.
- **Learning Reviews**: After success or failure, ask *what worked, what didn't, what will we do differently?* Focus on learning, not blame.

The Orchestra

Picture an orchestra.

- Engagement is the passion each musician brings to their instrument.
- Accountability is the discipline of following the score and keeping time.

With passion alone, the result is noise. With discipline alone, the performance is robotic. With both, the music transcends – moving not just the performers, but the audience.

That is the promise of engagement and accountability working in harmony.

When engagement fuels accountability and accountability deepens engagement, organizations build a performance culture that is both demanding and human. The next challenge is sustainability – ensuring leaders don't over-engineer connection but create rhythms that last. That is where **Pulse Engagement** comes in.

Pulse Engagement – Smarter, Not Harder

In the rush to boost engagement, many leaders fall into a trap: they try to do more of everything. More surveys. More check-ins. More town halls. More team-building events.

What begins as well-intentioned effort turns into exhaustion. Engagement fatigue sets in, and the very people leaders are trying to energize start to disengage. One employee at a leading bank described it perfectly:

"We were so busy filling out engagement surveys, we didn't have time to actually engage with each other."

The paradox is clear: the harder leaders push for connection, the more people check out.

From Over-Engineering to Pulse Engagement

Engagement is not about volume. It is about rhythm. Too little attention, and people feel invisible. Too much, and they feel smothered. The goal is not constant effort but consistent pulses – signals of care, recognition, and direction delivered at the right moments.

Pulse Engagement is the art of timely, authentic, and sustainable connection. Instead of exhausting people with scripted programs, leaders offer small, meaningful touchpoints that keep energy alive without overwhelming teams.

The Science Behind the Pulse

Psychology and neuroscience reveal two critical truths:

1. **Intermittent reinforcement is powerful.** Recognition and feedback matter most when they are unexpected and genuine, not routine and mechanical.
2. **Humans thrive on steady signals of belonging.** Small, consistent moments of attention create safety and trust. Over-saturation, on the other hand, creates noise, stress, and cynicism.

In short: **engagement is a pulse, not a flood.**

The Three Practices of Pulse Engagement

1. Spontaneous Praise: The Surprise That Builds Loyalty

- **What it is:** Recognition that's immediate, unplanned, and tied to a specific behaviour or outcome.
- **Why it matters:** Immediate praise strengthens the neural pathways connected to the behaviour, reinforcing it for the future. People feel most valued when their effort is noticed without prompting.
- **How to use it:** Notice small but meaningful contributions. Keep praise brief, authentic, and timely.

Leader Tip: Commit to three spontaneous praises each week.

2. Informal Check-Ins: Small Moments That Signal Care

- **What it is:** Quick, unstructured conversations about well-being or progress – outside formal one-on-ones.
- **Why it matters:** Builds psychological safety and prevents problems from festering. Shows employees they are valued as humans, not just producers.
- **How to use it:** Ask simple, open questions: *"How's your week going?"* or *"What's been the best part of your work this month?"*

Leader Tip: Dedicate 10–15 minutes weekly to "wander" – virtually or physically – checking in with 2–3 people.

3. Real-Time Feedback: The Accelerator of Learning

- **What it is:** Immediate, actionable feedback on behaviour, delivered as close to the event as possible.
- **Why it matters:** Strengthens the connection between action and impact, helping people adjust quickly. Prevents frustration and builds a growth culture where feedback is normalized.
- **How to use it:** Use the **SBI Formula** – *Situation → Behaviour → Impact.* For example: *"In today's meeting (situation), you asked sharp follow-ups (behaviour), which helped the team clarify priorities (impact)."*

Leader Tip: Ask for permission before giving sensitive feedback: *"Can I share a quick thought about that call?"*

Think of leadership like tending a garden:

- Spontaneous praise is like watering – small, regular boosts that help things grow.
- Informal check-ins are like pruning – gently shaping growth and removing friction.
- Real-time feedback is pulling a weed early – addressing issues before they take root.

Get all three right, and the team thrives with resilience, colour, and yield.

Supporting Tools to Scale Pulse Engagement

- **Short Weekly Surveys**: Replace long annual surveys with 2–3 pulse questions like *"How are you feeling this week?"* or *"What's one thing that's working well/not working well?"* Share insights openly and act visibly on results.
- **Leader Walk-Arounds**: Spend 15 minutes weekly in informal spaces – on the floor or in a virtual stand-up. Listen 80% of the time, speak 20%.
- **Shout-Out Channels**: Create digital spaces in Slack, Teams, or Yammer for peer appreciation. Prompts like *"Who helped you this week?"* keep gratitude flowing horizontally, not just top-down.

Pulse Engagement at a Fast-Growth Startup

At a Series B startup, engagement scores were dipping. Teams felt over-surveyed, all-hands meetings were stiff, and recognition programs felt forced.

The leadership team reset by:

- Replacing monthly surveys with two weekly pulse questions.
- Starting team meetings with "gratitude rounds."
- Having leaders do biweekly walk-arounds.
- Shifting all-hands to casual AMA (Ask Me Anything) formats.

The result: engagement rebounded, turnover dropped, and employees reported feeling more connected – not more managed.

The Heartbeat

Engagement is like a heartbeat.

- A steady, healthy pulse keeps the body energized and resilient.
- Erratic or excessive beats create strain.
- Flatlines – silence – are deadly.

Leaders who master pulse engagement don't exhaust their teams. They energize them.

Pulse Engagement reminds us that sustainability matters more than intensity. The goal is not to overwhelm people with constant noise but to provide steady rhythms of clarity, care, and recognition. When engagement becomes a pulse woven into daily leadership, it no longer feels like an initiative. It becomes the lifeblood of culture.

Engagement as the Pulse of Leadership

Engagement is often mistaken for cheerleading or enthusiasm – a flash of energy, a boost in morale. But true engagement is quieter and deeper. It's not a program or initiative. It's the daily rhythm of how leaders make people feel: seen, safe, trusted, and inspired.

We've explored what drives that rhythm – not perks, but purpose. Not pressure, but clarity. Not control, but connection. When people resist, it's rarely because they're unwilling. More often, it's because they feel unseen, uncertain, or alone.

Engagement begins when leaders stop pushing harder and start listening more. When they recognize not just output, but effort. When they create space for voice, for meaning, for shared progress. As we saw through stories like Sarah's and Maria's, even small shifts in leadership behaviour can spark profound change.

Engagement is not something you deliver. It's something you cultivate.

It lives in the formula:

Clarity + Autonomy + Recognition + Progress = High Engagement.

But it breathes through rhythm – the pulse of praise, the beat of check-ins, the feedback that keeps the system alive. And when it's working, leadership becomes something more than direction. It becomes music, growth, and motion.

The Leadership Imperative

The message is clear: Engagement isn't about doing more. It's about doing differently. Not about managing harder – but leading more humanly.

Leaders who understand this stop trying to force energy. They create the conditions where energy emerges on its own – through trust, meaning, and shared ownership. They don't ask, *Are people compliant?* They ask, *Do people care?*

Final Image: The Conductor, the Gardener, the Heartbeat

To lead with engagement is to wear three roles at once:

- The **conductor**, who shapes individual passion into shared harmony.
- The **gardener**, who creates the conditions where growth feels inevitable.
- The **heartbeat**, whose steady rhythm sustains the life of the team.

When leaders embody these roles, teams don't just perform – they flourish.
They don't just navigate change – they grow stronger because of it.
Because in the end, engagement isn't a part of the culture.

It is the culture.

Pause and Reflect

As you close this chapter, look at the energy behind execution in your teams and ask yourself:

- Are my teams engaged as co-owners of outcomes, or are they merely compliant executors of tasks?
- Where does motivation wane – and what systems (or lack thereof) might be draining it?
- How often do I listen with the intent to act, not just to respond?
- Where am I celebrating individual heroics instead of collective ownership?
- What would change if engagement became a daily leadership practice rather than an annual HR exercise?

Next Step on the Journey

Engagement is the spark that turns execution from obligation into ownership. It's the difference between a team that "has to" deliver and one that wants to deliver. Plans give direction, accountability gives structure, and communication gives clarity – but engagement gives the will to keep going when the path gets steep.

Picture a campfire: planning is the wood, accountability the structure, and communication the spark – but without fuel, the fire dies. Engagement is that fuel – the belief, the connection, the sense of shared purpose that keeps the flame alive long after the initial spark. As you turn the page, remember that execution is not sustained by systems alone; it is sustained by people who feel seen, trusted, and invested. And as organizations grow, so must the framework that sustains them. The next chapter explores how PACE scales – from nimble startups to sprawling enterprises – without losing its soul.

CHAPTER SIX

Applying PACE to Your Leadership

Turning Framework into Rhythm

"Execution is not a destination – it is the daily rhythm leaders create."

The Step-by-Step PACE Implementation Strategy

The PACE model is not an abstract framework to admire – it is a **leadership operating system** to live. The real power of PACE lies in how leaders embed it into the pulse of their organizations: shaping conversations, structuring routines, and setting the emotional tone.

When leaders apply PACE consistently, transformation shifts from slogans to lived experience. Teams move from compliance to ownership, and organizations evolve from rigid hierarchies to cultures of execution.

At the core of PACE implementation are **five essential moves.** They are not steps to complete and move on from; they are reinforcing disciplines that create momentum when practiced together.

Move 1: Align Around the North Star

Every leader must begin with clarity. A North Star is more than a slogan; it is the compelling aspiration that directs energy and choices. When leaders skip alignment, teams chase multiple "priorities," creating noise instead of progress.

To align effectively:

- Define the North Star with simplicity and conviction.
- Translate it into a handful of strategic priorities.
- Ensure it is understood at every level, not just in boardrooms.

The true test of alignment is not whether leaders can state the vision, but whether employees across the organization can explain what it means for them in their roles.

Move 2: Design Cascading Systems

Strategy collapses when it remains abstract. Cascading is the discipline of turning bold goals into team-level objectives so that every person owns part of the whole.

To design cascading systems:

- Break enterprise goals into functional and team objectives.
- Make ownership explicit – no vague groups or committees.
- Keep lines of accountability visible through reviews and dialogues.

When done right, cascading eliminates the disconnect between lofty aspirations and daily activity. Every individual can see the thread connecting their work to the organization's greater ambition.

Move 3: Model Leadership Behaviours

No system survives poor modelling at the top. Leaders are culture carriers; their actions speak louder than policies or playbooks. PACE requires leaders to set the tone by acting first and expecting second.

To model effectively:

- Demonstrate accountability by admitting mistakes openly.
- Invite feedback before demanding it.

- Recognize contributions consistently.

When leaders live the values they preach, trust grows. Teams follow not because they are told to, but because they want to.

Move 4: Embed Routines and Rituals

Change is fragile unless it becomes habitual. Routines are the scaffolding that sustain transformation. When leaders embed rituals of planning, accountability, communication, and engagement into daily and weekly rhythms, execution becomes second nature.

To embed routines:

- Establish a cadence of meetings that are short, purposeful, and consistent.
- Build recognition into weekly rhythms rather than annual ceremonies.
- Create forums where progress, obstacles, and learning are visible and shared.

Consistency matters more than intensity. One inspiring speech cannot achieve what a steady rhythm of aligned practices will.

Move 5: Measure and Adjust

PACE is not about perfection; it is about adaptation. Even the best plans falter if leaders cling to them rigidly. The fifth move is the discipline of listening, learning, and evolving without abandoning the framework.

To measure and adjust:

- Review both outcomes and behaviours regularly.
- Share progress transparently to build trust.
- Treat every cycle as a chance to refine, not to assign blame.

This adaptive approach keeps transformation alive. Instead of collapsing under change fatigue, organizations refresh their energy by adjusting course with confidence.

The Rhythm of the Five Moves

These moves are not sequential checkboxes. They are a continuous rhythm:

- Alignment provides direction.
- Cascading distributes ownership.
- Modelling sets the cultural tone.
- Routines embed discipline.
- Adjustments keep the system alive.

Together, they turn PACE from a concept into a lived practice. Leaders who embrace this rhythm don't simply talk about execution – they make it visible, sustainable, and contagious.

The CEO's Guide

The CEO is the architect of transformation. No matter how talented the executives or how disciplined the managers, the tone for execution is set at the very top. A CEO's job is not only to articulate vision but to ensure that vision becomes the organization's shared operating system. PACE gives CEOs a framework for doing just that.

The CEO role in PACE is about **three big responsibilities**:

1. **Shaping and communicating the North Star.**
2. **Designing governance and culture that reinforce accountability.**
3. **Modelling vulnerability, learning, and consistency.**

1. Define and Communicate the North Star

A North Star is the CEO's most powerful lever. It creates clarity in the midst of complexity. Yet too many CEOs treat it as a speech or a slide deck rather than a daily reference point.

PACE requires CEOs to:

- Boil down the organization's long-term aspiration into three to five priorities that everyone can remember.
- Communicate those priorities repeatedly, across formats – town halls, executive sessions, frontline visits.
- Reinforce the North Star not just in what is said but in where resources, attention, and time are allocated.

When people see the CEO prioritizing and living the North Star, it shifts from words to reality.

2. Align Governance and Incentives

Vision without reinforcement is fragile. Governance is where many transformations stall – boards focus on financials, executives chase functional wins, and the link to culture is lost.

To apply PACE, CEOs must:

- Overhaul governance forums so they reinforce accountability, not just reporting.
- Ensure incentives reflect execution discipline and cross-functional success.
- Make leadership development a strategic priority, not a "nice-to-have."

The CEO role here is not to run every meeting but to ensure **the system itself drives alignment.**

3. Model Leadership Behaviours

The most overlooked power of the CEO is symbolic. Every action sends a signal: what is praised, what is ignored, what is punished, what is tolerated. PACE leaders understand that they are **culture carriers in chief.**

That means:

- Owning mistakes publicly, showing that accountability is safe.
- Asking more questions than giving answers, showing humility.
- Recognizing effort and progress consistently, showing engagement.

When the CEO demonstrates vulnerability, it cascades courage down the system.

When the CEO shows accountability, it legitimizes accountability everywhere else.

The First 90 Days as a CEO on PACE

To make PACE real, CEOs should structure their first 90 days as a launch pad.

Day 0–30

- Announce a "state of execution" assessment to surface where planning, accountability, communication, and engagement are weak.
- Share initial reflections with transparency.

Day 30–60

- Build a coalition of PACE champions – cross-functional leaders who will model and cascade the framework.
- Begin visible changes in governance routines (shorter, more focused meetings; clear decision rights).

Day 60–90

- Communicate the PACE journey widely – town halls, newsletters, floor walks.
- Make early symbolic moves (recognizing a manager for modelling accountability, reshaping one board meeting around learning rather than reporting).

These first moves matter because they show the organization that PACE is not another initiative. It is the way leadership will now operate.

Common Pitfalls for CEOs

1. **Treating PACE as an HR program.**
   When execution is delegated to a staff function, it never takes root.
2. **Communicating once and going silent.**
   Repetition builds belief; silence breeds cynicism.
3. **Over-focusing on financial results.**
   PACE is about execution discipline. Financials matter, but they are lagging indicators.

The CEO's Mirror

- Am I personally visible as the architect of PACE, or am I outsourcing it?
- Do my words, incentives, and actions consistently reinforce our North Star?
- Where have I modelled vulnerability and accountability in the last month?
- What signals am I sending – intentionally or unintentionally – about what truly matters here?

In PACE, the CEO is not just a visionary. They are the chief execution architect. Their power is not only in setting direction but in **designing a system where execution thrives.** When CEOs embody PACE, the rest of the organization doesn't see it as optional. They see it as the way we do things here.

The Executive's Guide

If the CEO is the architect, executives are the **engineers and bridge builders**. They connect vision with execution, strategy with resources, and functions with one another. Without disciplined executives, even the clearest vision fragments into silos.

Executives sit at the critical intersection of **strategy, resources, and people**. Their role in PACE is to ensure that the North Star becomes more than rhetoric. They translate it into actionable plans, coordinate across divisions, and coach the next layer of leaders who will carry it forward.

1. Translate Strategy into Action

Executives often make the mistake of assuming strategy speaks for itself. In reality, every strategic decision requires translation into **clear objectives and shared accountabilities.**

PACE demands that executives:

- Convert strategic ambitions into functional and cross-functional goals.
- Create objectives that reflect not only "what we deliver" but also "how we

deliver."

- Eliminate ambiguity about ownership, ensuring that every initiative has a champion.

Translation is not clerical work; it is cultural work. When teams see executives take the time to clarify, they learn that execution matters as much as vision.

2. Break Silos with Cross-Functional Operating Rhythms

The greatest danger for executives is functional tunnel vision. Each department may achieve its own success while the organization as a whole fails. PACE reminds leaders that **execution dies at the boundaries.**

To counter this, executives must:

- Align functional strategies with enterprise priorities.
- Establish operating rhythms that bring functions together – monthly or quarterly steering reviews, biweekly huddles, and joint problem-solving forums.
- Use these forums to surface interdependencies, unblock shared initiatives, and prevent finger-pointing.

When cross-functional rhythms are in place, accountability no longer stops at the department door. It extends across the entire customer or value chain.

3. Allocate Talent and Resources to Priorities

Resources tell the truth about strategy. If budgets, teams, and talent reviews don't align with the stated North Star, people quickly conclude that priorities are lip service.

Executives applying PACE must:

- Audit resource allocation against priorities.
- Redirect funding, talent, and time toward transformation goals.
- Ensure that high-potential leaders are placed in roles critical to execution, not sidelined by politics or tradition.

Every shift in resource allocation sends a message: this is what truly matters.

4. Coach the Next Level of Leaders

Executives do not lead transformation by themselves – they **multiply leadership capacity** by coaching those below them.

This means:

- Mentoring managers on how to drive accountability without fear.
- Helping emerging leaders communicate transparently and clearly.
- Creating safe spaces for candid conversations about execution struggles.

PACE recognizes that strategy dies not because of intent but because of leadership gaps at the middle. Executives who actively coach fill that gap.

The First 90 Days as an Executive on PACE

A disciplined executive approaches the first three months not as a period of observation but as a **period of activation.**

Weeks 1–4

- Map where execution is breaking down across functions.
- Listen deeply to frontline concerns and identify bottlenecks.

Weeks 5–8

- Set joint accountabilities across teams.
- Launch a cross-functional huddle rhythm to address interdependencies.

Weeks 9–12

- Publicly celebrate examples of cross-functional wins.
- Begin coaching managers on PACE practices – clarity, accountability, communication, and engagement.

By the end of 90 days, executives should have created both structure and signal: structure through operating rhythms, and signal by demonstrating that cross-functional collaboration is valued and recognized.

Common Pitfalls for Executives

1. **Prioritizing functional wins over enterprise wins.**
   When the scorecard is dominated by silo metrics, shared outcomes suffer.
2. **Confusing governance with alignment.**
   More meetings don't equal better execution. Without shared priorities, governance is a ritual without results.
3. **Failing to coach managers.**
   Delegating execution downward without equipping managers creates burnout and disconnection.

The Executive's Mirror

- Have I translated our enterprise vision into clear, actionable goals for my area?
- Do I spend as much time on cross-functional priorities as I do on functional wins?
- Have I created rhythms where functions coordinate rather than compete?
- In the last month, how have I invested in the growth of next-level leaders?

Executives are the connective tissue of PACE. They ensure that the vision of the CEO is translated, resourced, and lived across the enterprise. Their value is not in owning all the answers but in **building the bridges where strategy meets execution.**

When executives embrace PACE, they stop leading functions in isolation and begin leading as part of an integrated whole. That shift is what makes transformation stick.

The Manager's Guide

If CEOs are architects and executives are engineers, managers are the **builders on the ground.** They are closest to where strategy meets daily work. Their role in PACE is critical because no matter how well-crafted a plan is at the top, it lives or dies in the way managers activate it with their teams.

Managers are more than conduits; they are **culture shapers.** Every meeting they run, every conversation they hold, every recognition they offer communicates what execution looks like in practice. PACE gives managers a framework to turn broad direction into lived discipline.

1. Translate Goals Into Daily Clarity

Managers are the interpreters of vision. A team member rarely interacts with the CEO, but they interact with their manager daily. If clarity doesn't flow here, it doesn't flow anywhere.

PACE expects managers to:

- Translate high-level goals into daily and weekly priorities for their teams.
- Revisit priorities often, making space to recalibrate when circumstances shift.
- Help each team member connect their contribution to the larger mission.

When managers provide clarity, confusion is replaced with confidence.

2. Build Accountability Into Team Rhythms

Accountability at the manager level is not about monitoring activity; it is about ensuring ownership of outcomes.

To apply PACE, managers must:

- Hold regular check-ins that focus on commitments and progress, not just problems.
- Encourage peer accountability within the team by making deliverables visible.
- Balance firmness with fairness – holding people to standards while removing obstacles in their way.

In this rhythm, accountability becomes less about enforcement and more about shared pride.

3. Communicate With Transparency and Respect

Managers are the **voice of leadership** to most employees. When communication is inconsistent or opaque, trust erodes.

PACE communication at the manager level means:

- Explaining the "why" behind shifts in priorities.
- Sharing information quickly rather than hoarding it.
- Listening actively to concerns and surfacing insights upward.

Transparent managers create psychological safety. Their teams don't just receive orders; they feel included in the journey.

4. Create Engagement Through Recognition and Care

Engagement for managers is not grand gestures – it's **everyday signals.** A quick acknowledgment of effort, a question about someone's well-being, or a shout-out in a team meeting can be more powerful than corporate programs.

Managers applying PACE should:

- Recognize contributions promptly and specifically.
- Celebrate both progress and effort, not just final outcomes.
- Make space for belonging by ensuring every voice is heard.

Engaged managers multiply energy. Disengaged managers drain it.

The First 90 Days as a Manager on PACE

Managers who want to bring PACE to life should use their first 90 days as a reset with their teams.

Weeks 1–4

- Meet individually with team members to understand strengths, challenges, and aspirations.
- Clarify how team goals link to enterprise goals.

Weeks 5–8

- Establish regular check-ins focused on progress and ownership.
- Launch simple recognition practices – "win of the week," peer shout-

outs, or Friday reflections.

Weeks 9–12

- Adjust routines based on feedback.
- Demonstrate consistency – keeping meetings focused, honouring commitments, and celebrating follow-through.

By the end of 90 days, teams should feel both clearer on expectations and more connected to one another.

Common Pitfalls for Managers

1. **Confusing busyness with progress.**
   Activity without clear outcomes leads to burnout.
2. **Over-controlling instead of empowering.**
   Micromanagement stifles ownership and creativity.
3. **Avoiding tough conversations.**
   Fear of conflict undermines accountability and fairness.
4. **Neglecting recognition.**
   When effort goes unnoticed, disengagement creeps in.

The Manager's Mirror

- Have I helped each team member see how their work connects to our larger mission?
- Do my routines encourage ownership or dependency?
- Am I communicating transparently, even when the news is difficult?
- How often do I recognize contributions in specific, meaningful ways?

Managers are the multipliers of PACE. They carry the framework into the everyday – in stand-ups, one-on-ones, project reviews, and hallway conversations. Their power lies not in dramatic moves but in the steady reinforcement of clarity, accountability, communication, and engagement.

When managers embrace PACE, transformation ceases to be a top-down program. It becomes the lived experience of every team, every day.

PACE Self-Assessment Diagnostic

One of the greatest challenges leaders face is knowing **where they truly stand** in execution. Many overestimate their clarity, underestimate their blind spots, or confuse activity with progress. Without a mirror, growth is guesswork.

The **PACE Self-Assessment Diagnostic** provides that mirror. It allows leaders to evaluate how deeply Planning, Accountability, Communication, and Engagement are embedded in their leadership practice and organizational culture. This is not about perfection but about honest reflection – a map to help leaders move from intention to mastery.

The Four Dimensions of PACE

Every organization expresses PACE differently, but the maturity of execution can be assessed across four levels:

1. **Emerging** – Awareness exists, but practices are inconsistent.
2. **Developing** – Systems are in place, but discipline is fragile.
3. **Performing** – Practices are embedded, consistent, and visible.
4. **Mastering** – PACE has become the organization's DNA; it drives culture and results seamlessly.

1. Planning Maturity

- **Emerging:** Goals are broad statements; plans are reactive, often rewritten when crises hit.
- **Developing:** Leaders create structured plans but struggle with cascading; teams often lack clarity on their role.
- **Performing:** Planning is adaptive; rolling cycles and scenario thinking guide execution; every team knows its priorities.
- **Mastering:** Planning is institutionalized; it balances long-term direction with short-term agility; the entire organization aligns to a shared rhythm.

Ask Yourself

- Do my people know how their work links to our strategic priorities?
- How often do we revisit and adjust our plans with agility?

2. Accountability Maturity

- **Emerging:** Accountability is equated with blame; mistakes are hidden.
- **Developing:** Leaders emphasize ownership but still default to top-down monitoring.
- **Performing:** Accountability is peer-driven; people own outcomes and admit missteps openly.
- **Mastering:** Accountability is cultural; it is seen as commitment, not control, and is modelled at every level.

Ask Yourself

- Do I create safety for my team to admit mistakes without fear?
- When ownership breaks down, do I address it swiftly and fairly?

3. Communication Maturity

- **Emerging:** Information is siloed; messages are delayed or watered down.
- **Developing:** Leaders push information downward but rarely invite feedback upward.
- **Performing:** Communication is two-way; leaders share transparently and listen actively.
- **Mastering:** Communication is systemic; truth flows across levels and functions without fear or filtering.

Ask Yourself

- Do I share context as openly as I share instructions?
- How consistently do I ask and act on feedback from my team?

4. Engagement Maturity

- **Emerging:** Engagement is treated as a perk or a program; leaders assume motivation is personal.
- **Developing:** Leaders experiment with recognition and team-building, but practices are inconsistent.
- **Performing:** Engagement is embedded in routines; recognition, inclusion, and care are everyday practices.
- **Mastering:** Engagement is cultural; people feel valued, trusted, and connected, even in times of disruption.

Ask Yourself

- How often do I recognize effort as well as outcomes?
- Do my team members feel they belong, or do they feel replaceable?

How to Use the Diagnostic

1. **Self-Reflection:** Leaders assess their current maturity honestly across each PACE dimension.
2. **Team Dialogue:** Use the diagnostic as a discussion tool in leadership forums, comparing perspectives.
3. **Growth Mapping:** Identify one or two dimensions to elevate in the next quarter; avoid trying to "fix everything at once."
4. **Re-Assessment:** Return to the diagnostic every 90 days to track progress and course-correct.

The diagnostic is not a scorecard. It is a compass. It doesn't grade leaders; it guides them. The purpose is not to label but to illuminate the path forward.

The question is not *"Where are we?"* but *"Where do we want to be – and what deliberate actions will get us there?"*

Scaling PACE – Large Organizations vs Startups

PACE is universal, but it is not uniform. The same framework lands differently depending on context. A multinational enterprise with thousands of employees cannot apply PACE in the same way as a founder-led startup racing to capture market share. Both need discipline, but the rhythms, cultural levers, and pace of application must adapt.

This section explores how PACE can be scaled in two contrasting worlds: **large organizations** and **startups.** Think of it as two mini-playbooks – each shaped by its own strengths, vulnerabilities, and cultural nuances.

The Large Organization PACE Guide

Large organizations carry weight – systems, history, and bureaucracy. This weight can be a stabilizer in times of disruption, but it also creates inertia. Leaders in such settings must apply PACE as a **renewal system** that cuts through silos and re-energizes culture.

How It Looks in Practice

- **Planning:** Instead of annual plans that gather dust, PACE requires rolling cycles. Leaders translate corporate strategies into cascaded objectives across divisions, ensuring alignment does not get lost in layers.
- **Accountability:** In big enterprises, accountability must move from being top-down to shared. Visible scoreboards and cross-functional steering forums help prevent blame games.
- **Communication:** Transparency is critical. Large organizations must fight the instinct to filter messages as they travel down. CEOs and executives need to model direct, unvarnished communication.
- **Engagement:** With thousands of employees, individual touchpoints may seem impossible. Yet engagement can scale through rituals: recognition programs, peer shout-out systems, and storytelling that reinforces belonging.

Short-Guide for Large Enterprises

1. Launch quarterly "PACE Reviews" where strategy, execution progress, and cultural signals are discussed together.
2. Establish cross-functional huddles that resolve interdependencies before they become bottlenecks.
3. Use storytelling – case studies from teams that live PACE – to inspire replication across layers.
4. Create visible rituals of recognition to rehumanize scale.

Cultural Nuance

The challenge is not inventing new systems but simplifying existing ones. In large organizations, leaders must prune bureaucracy, reframe governance, and focus energy on what truly matters. PACE works best when it becomes the antidote to complexity.

The Startup PACE Guide

Startups thrive on speed and improvisation. Their risk is not bureaucracy but chaos: energy without alignment, passion without process. For them, PACE is not a renewal system but a **stabilizing backbone** that channels creativity into execution.

How It Looks in Practice

- **Planning:** Startups must avoid the trap of chasing every shiny opportunity. PACE anchors them to a small set of non-negotiables, while still allowing for pivots.
- **Accountability:** In small teams, accountability is personal and visible. Leaders need to ensure commitments are explicit and tracked, not assumed.
- **Communication:** With flat structures, informal chatter dominates. PACE helps leaders formalize key communication without strangling spontaneity.
- **Engagement:** Startups thrive on passion but risk burnout. Leaders must build micro-rituals – daily stand-ups, gratitude rounds, or simple recognition practices – that protect energy and belonging.

Short-Guide for Startups

1. Begin every quarter by identifying three priorities and three only – align all activity to them.
2. Create lightweight routines: daily stand-ups, weekly retrospectives, and monthly founder check-ins.
3. Recognize contributions in the moment – don't wait for formality.
4. Use transparency as a cultural glue: share wins, struggles, and pivots openly.

Cultural Nuance

The challenge for startups is not lack of energy but lack of discipline. PACE ensures that speed does not become waste, and that passion does not collapse into burnout. When applied early, PACE becomes the DNA of culture before bad habits set in.

Integration: Two Contexts, One Discipline

Whether in the boardroom of a multinational or the co-working space of a startup, PACE adapts. It is not about applying every ritual the same way but about holding the same disciplines: clear planning, real accountability, transparent communication, and authentic engagement.

- In large organizations, PACE simplifies and renews.
- In startups, PACE stabilizes and sustains.

Both contexts prove the same point: **PACE is not a size-specific tool but a leadership operating system.** Its principles scale because they touch the fundamentals of human execution.

PACE in Crisis Leadership

Crisis is the ultimate test of leadership. It compresses time, magnifies fear, and exposes weaknesses in systems that once seemed stable. Plans unravel, communication falters, accountability blurs, and engagement suffers.

But a crisis does not have to paralyze an organization. Handled well, it can strengthen trust, sharpen focus, and accelerate alignment. What makes the difference is not charisma or improvisation, but disciplined use of the right framework. PACE provides that discipline.

When applied to crisis situations, PACE becomes a **stabilizing compass** – helping leaders think clearly, act decisively, and sustain the human energy required to endure.

The Crisis Guide: Four Adaptive Levers

1. Adaptive Planning: Navigate Without Paralysis

In a crisis, rigid plans collapse. What leaders need is adaptive planning: short, rolling horizons that balance immediate needs with emerging scenarios.

- Define **stabilization priorities** – what must be protected right now (cash flow, safety, customer continuity).
- Build rolling plans on 30-, 60-, and 90-day cycles.
- Create scenario buffers – best case, base case, and worst case – and rehearse responses.

Adaptive planning avoids the trap of endless reaction by providing a flexible but disciplined rhythm.

2. Shared Accountability: Stop the Blame Game

Crises often trigger finger-pointing. Teams retreat into silos, hoping responsibility will land elsewhere. This erodes trust and slows response.

PACE reframes accountability as shared responsibility. Leaders must:

- Make commitments explicit – "this is mine, this is yours, this is ours."
- Hold short daily or weekly check-ins where owners report status openly.
- Reinforce that accountability is not punishment but commitment to one another.

When accountability is shared, blame subsides and focus returns to collective problem-solving.

3. Transparent Communication: Replace Rumours With Truth

Silence in a crisis is deadly. In the absence of information, rumours fill the void, often faster than facts.

Leaders applying PACE must:

- Communicate early, even when they don't have all the answers.
- Share both bad and good news openly – credibility depends on candour.
- Use multiple channels to ensure the message reaches every layer.

The mantra is simple: *"If you're not talking, people are guessing. And their guesses will be worse than the truth."*

4. Fierce Engagement: Protect Energy and Morale

Crisis strains emotional reserves. People feel anxious, overextended, and unseen. Leaders who neglect engagement lose not just productivity but trust.

PACE helps sustain morale by:

- Recognizing effort daily, not just results.

- Checking in on well-being as much as performance.
- Celebrating small wins to keep hope alive.

Engagement in crisis is not about perks; it is about leaders making people feel valued when everything else feels uncertain.

A Crisis-Ready 30-Day Action Plan

Days 1–10

- Stabilize priorities.
- Set up crisis cadence (daily stand-ups, weekly leadership reviews).
- Communicate openly about what is known and unknown.

Days 11–20

- Launch rolling plans with scenario buffers.
- Clarify accountability lines – visible ownership for each initiative.
- Recognize and celebrate early adaptive responses.

Days 21–30

- Share lessons learned openly – what worked, what didn't.
- Reassess resources and redeploy as needed.
- Reinforce team resilience by celebrating progress.

This plan ensures that within one month, organizations shift from panic to rhythm.

Common Pitfalls in Crisis Leadership

1. **Over-centralization.** CEOs trying to control every decision suffocate speed.
2. **Withholding bad news.** Attempting to "protect" employees erodes trust when truth emerges later.
3. **Neglecting morale.** Overemphasis on tasks while ignoring people accelerates burnout.
4. **Sticking rigidly to old plans.** Inflexibility wastes energy on paths that no

longer fit the situation.

The Crisis Leader's Mirror

- When under pressure, do I cling to control or enable shared accountability?
- Am I transparent even when the news is uncomfortable?
- Do I provide rhythm and structure that calm panic, or do I fuel uncertainty?
- In the last crisis I faced, did I engage with empathy as much as urgency?

Crises do not demand perfection; they demand clarity, courage, and rhythm. PACE gives leaders a compass: adaptive planning, shared accountability, transparent communication, and fierce engagement.

Leaders who apply PACE in crisis not only survive disruption – they strengthen trust and resilience for the long road ahead.

Leading in Disruption and Uncertainty

Disruption is not a storm that passes. It is the climate we now live in. Technology evolves at breakneck speed, supply chains fracture without warning, consumer behaviour shifts overnight. For leaders, uncertainty is not the exception – it is the norm.

In such conditions, traditional leadership models that depend on stability collapse. Leaders who cling to rigid plans or outdated hierarchies risk irrelevance. What endures is not certainty, but the **discipline of adaptability.** This is where PACE becomes not just a framework for execution, but a **disruption accelerator** that channels turbulence into momentum.

The Disruption Accelerator Guide

PACE equips leaders to thrive in uncertainty by reframing disruption as an opportunity for reinvention. The playbook involves four adaptive practices:

1. Rolling Plans Instead of Fixed Blueprints

Long-term planning is fragile in volatile markets. What leaders need are **rolling horizons** that provide direction while leaving room to pivot.

- Anchor to a clear North Star, but revisit tactical plans every 90 days.
- Build flexibility into budgets, resources, and talent allocation.
- Encourage experimentation – let teams test, fail, and adjust quickly.

The discipline is not in sticking to the plan at all costs, but in **updating the plan without losing the mission.**

2. Resilient Accountability Instead of Fear-Driven Compliance

Uncertainty exposes weaknesses in ownership. When conditions shift, people may retreat into self-protection. Leaders must redefine accountability as resilience: a shared commitment to outcomes, even as the path changes.

- Make accountability forward-looking – focus on adapting, not punishing.
- Encourage teams to own both problems and solutions.
- Share responsibility for learning when experiments fail.

This kind of accountability transforms disruption into a collective challenge rather than an individual burden.

3. Radical Transparency Instead of Guarded Messaging

In disruption, information travels fast – and often inaccurately. Leaders who hide or delay communication create space for rumour and distrust.

- Share what you know, what you don't, and what you are doing to learn.
- Use multiple channels – digital updates, town halls, team check-ins – to keep truth flowing.
- Frame disruption as a shared reality, not a leader's secret to manage alone.

Transparency turns uncertainty from a fear-inducing void into a collective problem-solving exercise.

4. Cultural Engagement Instead of Transactional Motivation

When the ground is shifting, perks and slogans lose power. What sustains people is culture: trust, recognition, and shared purpose.

- Double down on rituals of belonging – gratitude rounds, cross-team recognition, moments of care.
- Recognize resilience, not just results.
- Involve employees in shaping responses to change; co-creation builds buy-in.

A culture of engagement ensures that people give their best not because they are forced to, but because they feel part of something larger than themselves.

Reinventing in Disruption

A mid-sized tech company faced a sudden market shift when a new competitor launched a breakthrough product. Instead of panicking, the leadership team applied PACE as a disruption accelerator:

- They pivoted planning to rolling 90-day sprints anchored to their North Star of customer trust.
- Accountability was shared through daily cross-functional war-room huddles.
- Communication was transparent – executives admitted uncertainty but shared learning weekly.
- Engagement was protected by celebrating experiments, even when results were inconclusive.

Within six months, the company launched its own innovative features, stabilized customer retention, and turned disruption into differentiation.

The Disruption Leader's Mirror

- Do I treat disruption as a threat to be endured, or a catalyst to be harnessed?
- Am I updating plans with agility, or clinging to outdated blueprints?
- Have I built a culture where accountability means resilience, not fear?
- How am I making transparency and engagement visible in times of uncertainty?

Surfing the Wave

Leading in disruption is like surfing. The waves are unpredictable, powerful, and sometimes overwhelming. You cannot control the ocean, but you can learn to ride it.

- **Planning is your balance board** – steady enough to stand, flexible enough to shift.
- **Accountability is your stance** – strong, grounded, and adaptable to changing waves.
- **Communication is your line of sight** – reading the swell before it breaks.
- **Engagement is your energy** – the stamina that keeps you paddling back for the next ride.

Surfers don't resist waves; they harness them. Likewise, leaders who embrace PACE in disruption turn uncertainty into motion, risk into opportunity, and turbulence into transformation.

PACE as a Living Operating System

Leaders often search for the one model that will guarantee transformation, the silver bullet that makes complexity disappear. But as we have seen throughout this chapter, leadership is not about single answers; it is about disciplined rhythms applied consistently. The strength of PACE lies not in being understood as a theory but in being lived as a daily operating system. Its true impact emerges when leaders at every level bring it to life in their unique roles.

At the top, CEOs anchor the rhythm – defining the North Star and setting the cultural tempo. Executives circulate the energy – connecting strategy to systems, breaking down silos, and aligning teams. Managers carry the beat daily – translating plans into the conversations, behaviours, and rituals that shape team momentum. When all three levels move in sync, the organization doesn't just execute. It comes alive.

PACE is resilient. It adapts across scale – providing clarity to the complex and structure to the scrappy. In crisis, it becomes a compass. In disruption, a stabilizer and an accelerator. It doesn't break under pressure – it beats stronger.

But to sustain that rhythm, leaders must practice it. That begins with honest reflection – not to judge, but to grow. The self-assessment isn't a scorecard. It's a mirror. Because progress in PACE isn't about perfection. It's about direction – and discipline. Across all contexts – from boardrooms to front lines, from startups to enterprises – one truth holds:

PACE is not a method to adopt. It's a culture to embody.

It connects vision to action. Strategy to trust. Leaders to people. And when practiced fully, it becomes the heartbeat of execution – steady, strong, and unmistakably human. The choice is not whether PACE works. The choice is whether to **live it** – or leave it on the page.

Pause and Reflect

As you close this chapter, look at how your systems are scaling with your growth and ask yourself:

- Where does PACE live only in slide decks—and where is it visible in daily rituals?
- Which one leadership behavior (mine) would most accelerate adoption this quarter?
- Where is accountability still a committee instead of a name?
- Which two standing meetings can we redesign next week to embody PACE (clarity, ownership, cadence)?

Next Step on the Journey

PACE moves from concept to culture when leaders model first, then mandate. Start small, start now: one clarified outcome, one named owner, one visible ritual, one short feedback loop. Momentum compounds through rhythm—not campaigns. Carry that rhythm forward as we tackle the recurring obstacles that derail even good implementations: the common transformation challenges that steal energy, scatter focus, and slow execution.

CHAPTER SEVEN

Breaking the Barriers

Overcoming Transformation Traps That Derail Execution

"A leader's job is not just to inspire the destination, but to design the path, clear the roadblocks, and walk it with the team."

The Brutal Truth About Transformation Failure

Imagine attempting open-heart surgery while the patient is running a marathon. The heart is exposed, fragile, and the stakes are life or death. But unlike a hospital, you can't pause the race. The patient must keep running – pumping blood, moving forward, keeping balance. That's what transformation feels like inside an organization.

Quarterly targets don't stop. Customers still demand service. Competitors don't wait politely on the sidelines. And employees? They still want clarity, stability, and hope, even as leaders rip up old systems and replace them with new ones.

Yet too often, leaders behave as if transformation happens in a sterile lab. They announce grand strategies, release glossy vision decks, and hold town halls filled with polished soundbites. But in the trenches, the reality is messy: silos, confusion, fear, and systems straining under pressure. Transformation isn't a project on a timeline. It's invasive, high-stakes surgery – on a moving, breathing, deeply human system.

And here's the inconvenient truth: statistically, most patients don't survive.

The Numbers Leaders Pretend Not to See

Leaders love to talk about disruption, agility, and "future-proofing." But the data tells a harsher story.

- **70% of transformations fail to meet their intended goals.** (McKinsey)
- **Only 30% of executives believe their change efforts succeed.** (BCG)
- **Less than 20% of employees** say their leaders communicate and manage change effectively. (Gartner)

Pause for a moment. Billions of dollars invested. Years of leadership workshops. Endless off-sites at luxury resorts. And still – seven out of ten transformations limp away bruised, broken, or unchanged.

This is not a side issue. It is a global leadership crisis. A silent epidemic of ambition wasted because leaders confuse vision with execution.

The Comfortable Lie: "People Resist Change"

Ask a CEO why transformation failed and you'll often hear the same refrain: *"People resist change."*

It's a seductive story. It blames human nature. It shifts responsibility to employees. It lets leaders off the hook. But it's also a lie.

Think about it:

- People camp overnight for the newest iPhone.
- Teams rally with energy when a new, inspiring leader takes charge.
- Entire industries pivot when survival is at stake.

People don't fear change. They fear confusion, half-truths, and leaders who don't walk their own talk. What employees resist isn't change – it's **poorly led change.**

Resistance is not the disease. It's the symptom. The disease is leadership unpreparedness.

The Landmines Leaders Pretend Don't Exist

Most transformations don't collapse because of stubborn frontline employees. They collapse because leaders underestimate the terrain. They walk into battlefields blind to the landmines beneath their feet.

What do these landmines look like?

- Leaders who overestimate readiness and assume a speech equals alignment.
- Leaders who underestimate the emotional toll of change, mistaking smiles for buy-in.
- Leaders who skip the cultural groundwork, treating transformation as a strategy deck rather than a human journey.
- Leaders who chase ambitious targets without the scaffolding of realistic execution systems.
- Leaders who communicate in soundbites, not substance – leaving people inspired for a day and confused for a year.

This is leadership by assumption. By ego. By denial. And like a surgeon who ignores the risk of infection, it poisons the operation before the first incision.

The Cracked Foundation

Picture a skyscraper under construction. The renderings are breathtaking. Investors are impressed. The media celebrates progress. The steel rises high, floor by floor.

But deep below, the foundation is cracked. At first, the cracks are invisible. The structure looks solid. Progress appears real. But as the weight increases, the fractures widen. Stress creeps in. Then, one day, the skyscraper crumbles.

This is what happens in most organizations.

The vision is bold.
The decks are polished.
The timelines are aggressive.

But the foundation – **Planning, Accountability, Communication, and Engagement** – is fractured.

The result isn't failure because the building was impossible. The result is collapse because leadership skipped the groundwork.

Why the Old Playbook Fails

Traditional change management loves its artifacts: checklists, Gantt charts, town halls, "change champions." They look reassuring. They feel structured. But they are incomplete.

They ignore the hidden human and systemic factors that decide success or failure:

- Is there cultural alignment beyond slogans?
- Do people understand *why* change matters, not just *what* is changing?
- Are accountability systems owned with pride, or enforced with fear?
- Is engagement authentic, or just a performance staged for HR surveys?

Without tackling these realities, transformation becomes a theatre production: rehearsed lines on stage, chaos behind the curtain.

The Leadership Bottleneck

Here's the mirror most leaders avoid: organizations don't fail to transform. Leaders fail to lead transformation.

Research confirms the blind spots:

- Only **22% of leaders** feel confident they can handle the people side of change.
- Over **65% admit** they underestimate the emotional toll on teams.

The problem isn't incompetence. It's blindness. Leaders are rewarded for short-term metrics, trapped in firefighting, disconnected from frontline realities, and over-reliant on consultants to carry the load.

This creates a dangerous gap: strategic ambition soaring in boardrooms while organizational readiness limps along on the ground.

Reframing the Narrative: Resistance vs. Readiness

If you remember one truth, let it be this: transformation failure is not an employee problem. It is a **readiness problem.**

Resistance surfaces when:

- Vision is unclear.
- Communication is inconsistent.
- Leadership behaviour contradicts the message.
- People feel stripped of ownership rather than empowered.

Flip the script. When readiness is addressed – through structured planning, shared accountability, radical transparency, and genuine engagement – resistance evaporates. Change becomes not a threat, but a cause worth rallying around.

A Wake-Up Call for Leaders

True transformation leadership begins with humility. With facing landmines instead of pretending they don't exist. With building readiness, not assuming it.

It demands:

- Rigorous planning that goes beyond pretty charts.
- Accountability that fosters ownership, not fear.
- Communication that enlightens, not confuses.
- Engagement that connects to purpose, not perks.

This is why the **PACE Model – Planning, Accountability, Communication, Engagement** – exists. It's not another framework for slides. It's a cultural operating system that prevents your skyscraper from collapsing under its own weight.

At the end of the day, leaders face a choice.

You can cling to the comforting myth: *"People resist change."*
Or you can embrace the uncomfortable truth: *"People resist poorly led change."*

The first fuels excuses. The second fuels growth.

Transformation is not optional. The world will demand it, whether you're ready or not. But failure? Failure is optional.

Pre-Implementation Pitfalls – The Seeds of Failure Are Sown Early

If transformation is surgery on a moving patient, then pre-implementation is the diagnosis phase. Get it wrong here, and it doesn't matter how skilled your surgeons are—the operation is doomed before the scalpel even touches the skin.

Here's the brutal truth: most transformations implode before they even start. Not because teams are unwilling or incompetent, but because leaders plant the seeds of failure in the earliest stages—often without realizing it. These seeds don't look dramatic. They don't announce themselves in headlines or shareholder reports. They're subtle, quiet, invisible... and lethal.

Let's dissect the five most common pre-implementation pitfalls that silently sabotage transformation before it even leaves the runway.

1. Lack of Clear Vision – The Silent Momentum Killer

If you cannot describe where you're going in one crisp, human sentence, you're not ready to lead transformation. Full stop.

And yet, clarity is shockingly rare. A Bain & Company study found that only **31% of employees can accurately articulate their company's strategic vision**. Even worse, many senior leaders can't either. They cloak vagueness in buzzwords:

- *"We're becoming future-ready."*
- *"We're driving digital excellence."*
- *"We're fostering customer-centric agility."*

It sounds visionary. It means nothing.

A leading insurance firm's CEO declared a bold shift toward *"digital leadership and customer-first culture."* Consultants were hired, roadmaps printed, and town halls held. Six months later, paralysis set in.

- IT pursued blockchain experiments.
- Marketing launched flashy apps.
- Operations automated processes without integration.

The result? Fragmentation, frustration, and failure. Not because the vision was wrong, but because it was never defined in the first place.

Lesson: If your people can't picture success, they cannot build it. Vision isn't an art project—it's an operating system.

2. Leadership Inconsistency – The Readiness Killer

Transformation begins at the top, but inconsistency also begins there. When leaders send mixed signals, they don't just confuse teams; they obliterate trust.

According to McKinsey, organizations with aligned, consistent leadership are **5.3 times more likely to succeed in transformation**. Yet in practice, alignment is rare:

- The CEO preaches bold change.
- The CFO quietly blocks investment.
- Line managers whisper doubts.
- Senior leaders contradict each other in meetings.

At a software firm, the CEO championed agile transformation. Sprints, empowerment, rapid iteration. Meanwhile, the COO clung to rigid hierarchy. Every decision still required layers of approval. Middle managers were trapped in two conflicting realities.

Chaos ensued. Employees didn't resist change—they resisted schizophrenia.

Lesson: Inconsistent leadership doesn't just slow momentum; it poisons the cultural bloodstream.

3. Inaccurate Readiness Assessment – The False Start

Here's one of the most dangerous leadership delusions: mistaking agreement for readiness.

- Nodding heads in meetings? Not readiness.
- Bold vision statements? Not readiness.
- Consultant slide decks? Definitely not readiness.

A Gartner report revealed that **over 60% of change initiatives fail because leaders misjudge organizational readiness**. They see enthusiasm and confuse it with capability.

The "Readiness Reality Check"

Before launching transformation, leaders must confront uncomfortable questions:

- Do frontline employees actually understand why change is happening?
- Are middle managers equipped—and willing—to champion it?
- Are existing processes and culture aligned with the future state?
- Are emotional barriers like fear, fatigue, and cynicism being addressed?
- Do we truly have the resources, time, and bandwidth to execute?

Optimism at this stage is a silent killer. Brutal honesty is the only antidote.

4. Cultural Misalignment – The Invisible Saboteur

Peter Drucker's famous quip – *"Culture eats strategy for breakfast"*—remains undefeated. Leaders love to fantasize about innovative, risk-taking cultures, but rarely examine the one they already have. Worse, they assume culture will "catch up" once the new strategy launches. It doesn't.

PwC's Global Culture Survey found that **67% of leaders believe culture is critical to transformation, but only 35% actively align it**. That gap is where strategies go to die.

A pharmaceutical giant announced a transformation to become customer-centric and innovative. But decades of regulatory rigor had forged a culture of caution and consensus. When innovation labs opened, employees hesitated to experiment, managers clung to process, and fear of failure paralyzed teams.

The labs existed on paper. Innovation never took root.

Lesson: You cannot layer new strategy on top of old culture without fracture. Culture isn't a soft backdrop—it's the load-bearing wall.

5. Inadequate Resources – The Inevitable Breakdown

Here's a blunt truth: vision without resourcing is hallucination.

Yet many leaders starve transformation before it begins. They announce ambitious change, but withhold:

- Financial investment.

- Talent with new capabilities.
- Modern technology infrastructure.
- The most undervalued resource of all: time.

A McKinsey Global Survey reports that **over 50% of failed transformations cite inadequate resources as a root cause.** Underfunded change is not unfortunate—it is designed to fail.

A multi-brand retailer declared a digital customer experience revolution. The CEO announced it with fanfare. But budgets for data infrastructure, training, and change management were denied.

Legacy systems clashed with new apps. Employees burned out. Customer frustration soared. Transformation didn't fail from lack of ambition—it failed from lack of oxygen.

The Transformation That Never Stood a Chance

A leading telecom provider announced its "Future-Ready Network" initiative with great publicity. But beneath the PR glitter:

- The vision was vague. "Future-ready" meant different things to different teams.
- Leadership was fractured: CTO pushing digital, COO resisting disruption.
- No readiness assessment was conducted—assumptions ruled.
- The culture remained risk-averse.
- Budgets were slashed mid-initiative.

Eighteen months later: engagement hit record lows, market share fell, and the program was quietly "paused."

The truth: This company didn't fail to change. It failed to prepare for change.

The Pattern is Global—and Predictable

Across industries, continents, and company sizes, the pattern repeats:

Pre-Implementation Pitfall	Predictable Consequence
Lack of clear vision	Fragmented execution
Leadership inconsistency	Eroded trust

Readiness misjudgment	False starts, rework
Cultural misalignment	Change rejection
Inadequate resources	Burnout, frustration

The real question isn't whether these pitfalls exist in your organization. They do. The question is whether you have the courage to face them before it's too late.

You Can't Build on Quicksand

Think back to the skyscraper metaphor: a towering structure rising on a cracked foundation. It looks impressive, until stress fractures appear and collapse becomes inevitable.

That's transformation without preparation.

Preparation is not a luxury; it's the operating system of successful change. The seeds of failure are always sown early. But so are the seeds of success—planted by leaders willing to slow down, diagnose honestly, and lay the groundwork with ruthless clarity.

Because here's the myth-busting truth: transformation doesn't fail because "people resist change." It fails because leaders resist reality.

The Hidden Traps During Execution – When Momentum Collapses

Launching a transformation feels like strapping into a rocket. The decks are polished, the town halls are electric, and the leadership team nods in unison. There's applause, optimism, and the intoxicating sense that a new chapter has begun.

But then reality arrives. Execution is not a celebratory sprint. It's the battlefield where lofty ambitions meet organizational gravity. It's where structural cracks widen, where enthusiasm thins, and where even the most promising initiatives quietly lose steam.

The brutal truth is this: **most transformations don't fail in the boardroom; they fail in the trenches.** And the reason isn't that employees are stubborn or change-averse—it's that leaders underestimate the traps that lie between intention and impact.

Let's pull back the curtain on these traps. They are predictable, they are deadly, and they sabotage organizations not because they are invisible, but because leaders refuse to name them.

Trap #1: Resistance to Change – Symptom, Not the Disease

The go-to scapegoat is always the same: *"people resist change."* It's the corporate equivalent of blaming gravity for a crash. It feels rational, it lets leadership off the hook, and it avoids uncomfortable self-examination. But it's also wrong.

Resistance is not the disease; it's the fever. A visible symptom of deeper infections: poor communication, inconsistent leadership, fear of incompetence, cultural misalignment, and the exhaustion that comes from being dragged through one poorly run change after another.

McKinsey's research is damning: employees resist change **2.5 times more** when they feel uninformed or excluded. This isn't human stubbornness—it's leadership negligence.

People don't resist change when they feel empowered. They resist when change feels like theft—of competence, of control, of certainty. When a system rewrites their role overnight without explanation, when new technologies arrive without training, when leaders declare a new future but can't articulate what it means for the individual, resistance is rational.

Here's the disruptive truth: **people don't fear change; they fear loss.**

- Loss of competence: *"Will I still be good at my job?"*
- Loss of control: *"Will I have a say in how this unfolds?"*
- Loss of certainty: *"What happens to me next?"*

Leaders who dismiss resistance as "human nature" guarantee its persistence. Leaders who diagnose the root causes of resistance transform fear into fuel.

Trap #2: Silos Between Departments – Organizational Cholesterol

If resistance is the fever, silos are the hidden cholesterol clogging an organization's arteries. They accumulate quietly, go unnoticed for months or years, and then one day—during the strain of transformation—they trigger a heart attack.

Harvard Business Review reports that **72% of failed transformations cite lack of cross-functional collaboration** as a core factor. Yet many executives treat silos as annoyances, not existential threats.

Think of silos like cholesterol:

- You can't always see them.
- They build up slowly, disguised as "focus" or "ownership."
- They restrict the flow of information, trust, and accountability.
- Left unchecked, they choke the system until breakdown is inevitable.

Consider the launch of a new product at a software company. Engineering built a brilliant solution. But marketing wasn't involved early, sales didn't understand the technical depth, and customer support wasn't trained. On launch day, the product flopped—not because it lacked quality, but because silos killed coherence.

The uncomfortable truth: **silos don't just delay decisions—they destroy transformation.**

Trap #3: Poor Communication – The PACE Breakdown

Communication, the third pillar of the PACE framework, is not a nice-to-have during execution. It is oxygen. Without it, transformation suffocates.

But this is where most organizations falter. What begins as clear, confident messaging in the planning phase disintegrates during execution into rumours, conflicting updates, and corporate jargon so empty it borders on satire. PwC found that **55% of employees cite poor communication as the single biggest barrier to change.**

When leaders get lazy, communication becomes dangerous. Vague updates breed fear. Inconsistent messages erode trust. Overly polished corporate language widens the gap between leadership and the frontline.

Execution thrives on radical clarity:

- Clear what's changing.

- Clear why it's changing.
- Clear how people will be impacted.
- Clear how success will be measured.

Without this, the PACE model collapses, and so does execution.

Here's the disruptive truth: **silence and spin are not communication strategies; they're sabotage strategies.**

Trap #4: Operational Disruption – When Change Breaks the Business

Every transformation, by definition, disrupts. But disruption without design is recklessness. Leaders intoxicated by ambition often forget that while they're building the future, the present must still function. Customers still expect service. Teams still carry daily workloads. Operations cannot go dark for the sake of experimentation.

When operational safeguards are ignored, organizations face breakdowns that erode trust and destroy momentum: customer service collapses, productivity craters, employees burn out, and revenues nosedive.

This is why leaders need what I call the **Minimal Viable Disruption (MVD) model.** Borrowed from the world of product design, MVD asks leaders to sequence change in ways that test and stabilize before scaling:

- What must stay stable during early phases?
- How can new ways of working be tested in safe, small pilots?
- Where are buffers needed to absorb inevitable hiccups?

One retail chain learned this the hard way. Overnight, it digitized payments, automated checkout, and rolled out AI-driven stock management. The problem? Employees were untrained. Systems failed. Customers fled. Revenues tanked. The transformation wasn't paused because the vision was wrong–it was paused because the execution was reckless.

The truth is bold but simple: **change that breaks today for the sake of tomorrow destroys both.**

Trap #5: Overly Ambitious Goals – The Burnout Trigger

Leaders love to declare audacious targets. They believe ambition inspires. But there's a dark line between ambition and delusion. Unrealistic timelines don't inspire—they exhaust. They don't energize—they demoralize.

Bain & Company found that organizations with overly ambitious targets are **40% more likely to experience burnout and disengagement.** Burnout isn't a side effect of bad luck; it's a design flaw.

Take the healthcare provider that promised to digitize all patient records in twelve months. IT teams clocked 70-hour weeks, frontline staff revolted, and quality of care dropped. Eighteen months later, the project was half-finished and the best talent had quit. The vision wasn't flawed—the pacing was.

Ambition without realism doesn't just kill projects. It kills people's trust in leadership.

A Familiar Pattern: Paper-Perfect, Reality-Flawed

Here's the harshest truth of all: most transformations look perfect on paper. The strategy decks are award-worthy, the leadership alignment looks impressive, and the vision statements sparkle.

But reality doesn't play out on PowerPoint. Reality plays out in silos, in exhausted employees, in muddled communication, in operations buckling under strain. And when the crash comes, leaders rarely point the finger at themselves. They blame employees for resisting. They blame markets for shifting. They blame consultants for misguiding.

But the truth is obvious: **execution collapses because leaders ignored the traps.**

The Mid-Execution Health Check – A Tool Leaders Avoid

Most executives don't want to pause mid-flight. They fear it signals weakness, doubt, or indecision. But smart leaders know that stopping to check the engine doesn't slow the plane—it prevents a crash.

A **mid-execution health check** should ask blunt questions:

- Are silos shrinking or growing?
- Is communication still clear and two-way, or has it decayed into noise?
- Are operations stable, or is disruption undermining the business?

- Is resistance a reflection of human fear—or a mirror of leadership failure?
- Are targets realistic, or are we quietly burning people out?

The leaders who dare to ask these questions don't just protect momentum—they accelerate it.

Execution as the Leadership X-Ray

Execution doesn't lie. It strips away the polish of strategy decks and reveals the truth about leadership capability.

It is the X-ray that exposes structural fractures, cultural weaknesses, and blind spots leaders would rather ignore. It is also the crucible where trust is forged, small wins become momentum, and accountability deepens into ownership.

This is why execution is not the middle chapter of transformation. It is the battlefield where transformation either dies or becomes real.

Here's the challenge for every leader: stop blaming employees for resistance, stop pretending silos will self-correct, stop hiding behind vision statements, and stop overloading your teams with impossible goals. Execution is where leadership is tested, not theorized. It's where illusions collapse and reality demands courage.

And if you dare to lead here—with humility, discipline, and brutal honesty—you won't just survive execution. You'll transform through it.

The Post-Implementation Mirage – When Change 'Looks' Done But Isn't

The town hall applause fades. Consultants pack their bags. Dashboards glow green. Leaders breathe a sigh of relief. The project is "done."

This is the **post-implementation mirage**—a dangerous illusion where change looks complete but has barely begun. On the surface, transformation appears installed. Beneath the surface, however, the old culture lurks like weeds beneath freshly laid turf, waiting for the first chance to grow back through.

The truth is harsh: **transformation is not a project with an end date. It's a discipline.** The finish line leaders love to declare is actually just the starting line for sustaining new ways of working.

And yet, this mirage deceives countless organizations. Leaders confuse activity with integration, compliance with commitment, and installation with transformation. The result? Gains fade. Morale drops. Old habits reassert themselves. And what looked like victory quickly slides into regression.

Regression to Old Habits – The Brain's Default Setting

Humans are wired for comfort. Neuroscience shows it takes at least 66 days to establish a new habit—and far longer for an organization to hardwire change into its culture. Without reinforcement, people default to familiar routines, even if those routines were dysfunctional.

This is why so many transformations relapse. Daily huddles stop. Visual boards gather dust. Leaders retreat from visibility. And slowly, the organization drifts back to the very patterns it swore to abandon.

Consider the auto parts manufacturer that celebrated a lean transformation. Within six months, efficiency was up 15%. But leaders declared victory too early. Without ongoing reinforcement, frontline teams slipped back into old ways of working. Within a year, every efficiency gain had evaporated. **It wasn't defiance that killed the change—it was drift.**

The harsh truth: change doesn't collapse in one dramatic moment. It leaks away silently, one unreinforced behaviour at a time.

Lack of Engagement – The Silent Killer

During implementation, engagement feels electric. Leaders are visible. Communication is relentless. Recognition flows. Energy runs high because the stakes are high.

But once the "launch phase" ends, leaders retreat into strategy and the energy fades. Without visible reinforcement, teams slide from enthusiasm to exhaustion to indifference. And disengagement rarely announces itself loudly—it creeps in quietly.

Performance begins to dip. Accountability weakens. Innovation slows. Early adopters grow cynical, telling themselves, "We've seen this movie before."

Gallup data is sobering: **only 23% of employees globally report feeling engaged at work, even after major organizational change.** Leaders who assume engagement will sustain itself are deceiving themselves. **Engagement is not a project. It's a habit.** And when it fades, so does the transformation.

The Mirage Exposed: Sustainability Is the Real Measure

Here's the unfiltered reality: transformation is never measured at the kickoff, or even at the rollout. It's measured in the quiet months that follow. The question is not whether you launched the change, but whether the change survived the absence of spotlights.

This is where leaders must ask: **are we sustaining, or are we slipping?**

To answer honestly, you need a diagnostic. That's why I built the **Sustainability Scorecard**—a brutally simple tool to test whether your transformation is alive, or already decaying.

Sustainability Scorecard – Keeping Change Alive

Category	Key Questions	Red Flags
Behaviour Reinforcement	Are the new behaviours visible daily, not just in formal reviews?	Old routines creeping back in quietly.
Engagement Levels	Are employees energized, proud, and willing to advocate for the change?	Rising absenteeism, turnover, or cynicism.
Cultural Alignment	Do structures, rituals, and incentives reinforce the new culture?	Contradictory practices that signal "business as usual."
Leadership Visibility	Are leaders consistently modelling the change—even when it's inconvenient?	Leaders retreating to old habits or silence.
ROI Visibility	Are both hard metrics (performance, cost, growth) and human stories (trust, collaboration, innovation) clearly communicated?	Confusion, scepticism, or "we don't see the impact."

How to Use This:
Review it quarterly, not annually. Invite uncomfortable feedback from across levels. Treat any red flag as an early-warning system—not as a failure, but as a chance to reinforce before regression becomes irreversible.

Short-Termism – The Self-Sabotage of Quick Wins

Every boardroom wants results—fast. Investors, executives, and stakeholders demand proof that the transformation is "working." And so leaders chase quick wins.

But here's the paradox: the faster leaders chase early wins, the faster they abandon the deeper, cultural work that actually sustains change. Quick wins are not the problem—it's when they **replace** long-term reinforcement that they become sabotage.

The high-growth fintech that digitized aggressively is a perfect example. Processes were streamlined. Teams were restructured. Investors were dazzled. But within six months, burnout spiked, service quality fell, and customer churn rose. Leaders had declared victory, but they had not consolidated cultural and operational shifts. **They harvested the fruit before the roots took hold.**

Quick wins inspire confidence. But only if they are used to build momentum toward deeper transformation, not as substitutes for it.

The ROI Mirage – Metrics Without Meaning

Nothing drains transformation faster than failing to prove impact. If employees and executives can't see tangible results, belief erodes.

But here's the mistake leaders make: they measure only the hard numbers. Revenue. Cost savings. Productivity. These matter—but they're not enough. Transformation is sustained by a **dual ROI**:

- **Hard metrics** that prove financial value.
- **Human stories** that show cultural, behavioural, and emotional value.

One retail company understood this. After implementing a supply chain transformation, leaders didn't just share dashboards. They also told frontline stories: how warehouse teams redesigned workflows, how customer satisfaction rose, how small ownership moments sparked innovation.

The result? Employees believed in the transformation because they could feel it—not just see it. And executives doubled down with continued investment.

Lesson: People invest in what they can measure—and what they can feel. Without both, momentum fades.

Loss of Talent – The Burnout Fallout

Transformation demands energy. New systems, new skills, new ways of working. The human toll is enormous. And if leaders don't protect their people, the very talent that delivered the change will walk out the door.

This isn't theory–it's happening everywhere. One IT services firm executed a successful digital transformation–technically. But within a year, **30% of its top technical talent resigned.** Why? Burnout. Poor communication. Lack of recognition.

The bitter irony? The transformation succeeded on paper, but the organization couldn't sustain it without its people. Leaders celebrated the project and ignored the humans. And in doing so, they sabotaged the future.

The reality is this: **burnout is the hidden tax of poorly paced, poorly reinforced change.** If you don't pay attention to it, you'll pay for it in talent loss.

The Hidden Danger: Transformation Fatigue

Beyond burnout lies something even more insidious: fatigue. This isn't rebellion–it's resignation. People don't actively fight change; they simply stop caring.

Fatigue shows up as eye-rolls at new initiatives. Passive compliance. A culture of "just get through this." Leaders mistake this as buy-in because no one is openly resisting. But in truth, it's the death knell of transformation.

Fatigue arises when change is poorly paced, poorly reinforced, and poorly communicated. The antidote? Empathy, pacing, recognition, and relentless visibility. Leaders must celebrate milestones, sustain rituals, and stay present long after the launch is over. Because when leaders disappear, fatigue spreads like wildfire. And once fatigue takes hold, even the best-designed transformations collapse quietly.

Transformation Is Never "Over"

The most dangerous illusion in leadership is finality–the belief that change has a finish line. Transformation is not like building a house, where the final brick is laid and the work is complete. It is like tending a garden.

You plant seeds—new behaviours, systems, and rituals.
You nurture growth—reinforcement, recognition, and engagement.
You protect against weeds—regression, fatigue, and cynicism.
You adapt to seasons—market shifts, leadership transitions, crises.

The work is never "done." But that is the point. **Transformation is not an event—it is a permanent capability.**

The leaders who thrive are those who reject the mirage, embrace the grind of reinforcement, and understand this truth: the confetti is irrelevant. The culture you leave behind is the only scoreboard that matters.

The Leadership Blind Spots That Fuel These Challenges

"Transformation rarely fails because employees resist change. It fails because leaders resist the mirror."

Executives love to talk about disruption. They obsess over competitors, technology, markets, and customer shifts. But the most dangerous disruptions are not external—they are internal. They live in leadership blind spots.

The uncomfortable truth is this: **most transformations are sabotaged not by markets or employees, but by the unexamined biases of leaders themselves.** Leaders with the best of intentions can unknowingly create the very obstacles they're trying to dismantle.

They deliver polished speeches. They host off-sites. They craft vision decks that dazzle. And yet, when transformation crumbles, it's not because the workforce lacked discipline—it's because leadership operated under illusions.

The real enemy of transformation isn't resistance. It's delusion.

Blind Spot 1: The Overconfidence Trap

We tend to assume that experience immunizes leaders against mistakes. In reality, experience often blinds them. The **Dunning-Kruger effect**, which describes how people with limited knowledge overestimate their competence, doesn't vanish at senior levels—it mutates.

For seasoned leaders, it shows up as the illusion that "we've done this before, so we'll nail it again." Past success becomes a false predictor of future readiness. Overconfidence drives leaders to:

- Overestimate how prepared their organization is.
- Underestimate cultural resistance.
- Launch initiatives before systems, processes, or people are ready.

Take the telecom CEO who, emboldened by past wins, greenlit a sweeping digital overhaul. Warnings about legacy systems were brushed aside. The result? Customer backlash, technical chaos, and a 12-month delay.

The wake-up call: Confidence is not competence. Experience can be a liability if it blinds leaders to the unique realities of this transformation, in this moment.

Reflection Check: Where are you assuming readiness without evidence? When was the last time you validated assumptions with frontline data rather than boardroom optimism?

Blind Spot 2: Vision Without Operational Grounding

Vision is seductive. It inspires. It rallies. But vision without operational grounding is a trap—a shiny rocket without an engine.

Leaders intoxicated by their big-picture narrative often skip the messy details of execution. They assume teams will "figure it out." They conflate storytelling with system-building. The result? Inspiration without infrastructure.

Consider the retailer that announced an "Omnichannel Revolution." The vision thrilled stakeholders. But store operations, supply chain, and IT weren't prepared. Customers faced confusion, employees faced chaos, and the grand revolution was quietly scaled back.

Vision matters. But unless it is translated into:

- Detailed operational roadmaps.
- Realigned resources.
- Frontline capability-building.

...it is little more than theatre.

Reflection Check: Is your vision truly connected to ground-level capability, or is it a moonshot without a rocket?

Blind Spot 3: Neglecting Culture as a System

Many leaders talk about culture. Few lead it deliberately. They treat culture as atmosphere—something fuzzy, intangible, and separate from execution. But culture is not atmosphere; it's **infrastructure.**

Culture is the invisible operating system of the organization. It dictates how decisions are made, how people behave under pressure, and what behaviours are rewarded or punished. Ignore it, and your strategy will collapse.

Think of culture as software code. If your processes and structures are hardware, culture is the code that makes the hardware run. If the code is misaligned—risk-averse in a world that demands agility, hierarchical in a world that requires empowerment—your "hardware" will crash.

A global bank learned this the hard way. They declared an "agile transformation," launched new rituals, and restructured teams. But they ignored the deeply embedded culture of bureaucracy and compliance. Result? Agile in name, bureaucracy in practice. Projects stalled, and cynicism spread.

Reflection Check: Are you managing culture as intentionally as you manage budgets? Or are you leaving it to chance while expecting transformation to thrive?

Blind Spot 4: Treating Change as an Event, Not a Process

Leaders love milestones: kickoff launches, press releases, "go-live" dates. These moments create theater and energy. But they also create an illusion—that change has a finish line.

Transformation is not an event. It is a process. Declaring victory too early is one of the most dangerous blind spots in leadership. When leaders signal "mission accomplished," teams interpret it as permission to relax. Regression begins the next day.

A fast-growing tech firm executed a cultural reset, celebrated loudly at an all-hands, and then... stopped reinforcing it. Six months later, old power dynamics returned, employees grew cynical, and the "reset" became a temporary performance rather than a permanent shift.

Reflection Check: Are you treating transformation as a project with an end date—or as a capability that must be reinforced continuously?

Why These Blind Spots Persist

You might ask: Why do smart, well-meaning leaders keep falling into these traps? The answer lies in three forces:

1. **Cognitive Biases** – Leaders are human. They rely on shortcuts and assumptions, which blind them to inconvenient truths.
2. **The Leadership Bubble** – At the top, feedback is filtered. Leaders hear what people think they want to hear. This insulation amplifies illusions.
3. **Fear of Vulnerability** – Admitting uncertainty feels risky. Leaders hide blind spots instead of surfacing them, reinforcing the cycle of delusion.

Research consistently confirms this. A McKinsey study found only **16% of organizations rate their leaders as "very effective" at role-modelling the behaviours needed for transformation.** The gap isn't technical—it's perceptual. Leaders believe they're being clear. Employees remain confused. Leaders believe culture is aligned. Employees know it isn't.

This gap is not malicious—it's unconscious. And unconscious blind spots are the most dangerous of all.

Breaking the Blind Spot Cycle

The antidote to blind spots isn't more frameworks or dashboards. It's **ruthless self-awareness.** Leaders must disrupt their own assumptions as fiercely as they try to disrupt markets.

That means asking uncomfortable questions and inviting unfiltered feedback. It means modelling vulnerability, not invincibility. It means recognizing that leadership credibility is built not on the absence of mistakes, but on the willingness to own them.

Here's a practical tool to start:

PACE Leadership Blind Spot Check

Blind Spot	Self-Reflection Question	Red Flag Signal
Overconfidence Bias	Where am I assuming readiness without evidence?	Surprise resistance, failed rollouts
Vision Without Grounding	Is my vision backed by operational muscle?	Teams overwhelmed, targets missed
Neglect of Culture	How am I managing culture beyond slogans?	Misaligned values, hidden silos
Change as an Event	Am I treating transformation as done—or as ongoing?	Regression to old behaviours

The value of this tool isn't in the table itself. It's in the conversations it sparks. When leadership teams answer these questions candidly—and share answers openly with their people—they close the gap between perception and reality.

The Courage to See Clearly

The greatest threat to transformation isn't disruption, competition, or employee resistance. It's the illusions leaders carry unchallenged.

The courage to see clearly begins with this realization: **you are not immune to blind spots.** Your confidence, your vision, your cultural assumptions, your obsession with milestones—any of these can quietly sabotage the very change you're trying to lead.

Great leaders disrupt not just markets but themselves. They cultivate:

- Self-awareness over ego.
- Operational grounding over empty vision.
- Cultural stewardship over slogans.
- Enduring processes over event-driven theatrics.

Transformation is a mirror. It reflects not just the strength of your organization, but the honesty of your leadership. And only leaders willing to confront their own illusions can turn fragile projects into lasting change.

Breaking the Cycle —Anticipating and Neutralizing Challenges

"Most leaders manage transformation like firefighters. The best manages it like architects—they design out the fires before they ignite."

By now, we've explored the brutal realities of transformation: the staggering failure rates, the hidden landmines, the execution traps, the post-implementation mirages, and the leadership blind spots that quietly sabotage progress.

Here's the disruptive truth: **transformation challenges are not mysterious. They're predictable.** The tragedy is that most leaders act surprised when they appear. They stumble into the same traps their predecessors did, then blame "resistance," "the market," or "bad luck."

But transformation is not roulette. It's a pattern-driven discipline. When leaders anticipate risks early and equip themselves with the right tools, the odds shift dramatically. This is the difference between running a reactive "firefighting" transformation and leading a proactive, architected one.

That's where the **Toolkit** comes in. It isn't about adding more theory to your bookshelf. It's about arming leaders with **practical, real-world instruments** that surface risks early, neutralize landmines, and sustain change beyond the confetti of launch day.

The Transformation Risk Radar™ – Seeing the Landmines Early

Imagine walking through a battlefield littered with hidden landmines—unseen dangers buried beneath the surface. Most leaders stroll through transformation this way—blind to the hidden risks.

The **Transformation Risk Radar™** is your early detection system.

It maps the most common—and most dangerous—transformation risks at each stage of the journey:

Stage	Key Risks

Pre-Implementation	- Vague vision signals misalignment.- Leadership inconsistency erodes trust.- Readiness assumptions conceal gaps.- Cultural friction festers beneath the surface.- Resource shortfalls trigger early failure.
Execution	- Resistance is misdiagnosed as an "employee problem" rather than a leadership gap.- Departmental silos clog collaboration.- Communication deteriorates into noise or silence.- Operational disruption snowballs beyond control.- Ambitious targets crush morale.
Post-Implementation	- Old habits creep back in—unnoticed at first.- Engagement drains away silently.- Short-term wins mask long-term vulnerability.- ROI remains unproven—credibility erodes.- Top talent walks out the door.

Reflection Moment: Which quadrant of your radar is already blinking red? Be honest. If you don't know, that's your first blind spot.

The genius of the Risk Radar isn't in its categories—it's in its frequency of use. Leaders who run this scan quarterly can prevent derailments that others only diagnose after collapse.

Tool 1: The Alignment Audit – Cutting Through Vision Fog

Most visions fail not because they're uninspiring, but because they're unintelligible. "Future-ready." "Digital-first." "Customer-obsessed." These sound impressive in boardrooms but meaningless on the front line.

The **Alignment Audit** is brutally simple:

- Gather a cross-section of leaders, managers, and frontline employees.
- Ask each one: *"Can you articulate our transformation vision in one clear, human sentence?"*
- Compare answers.

If fewer than 70% say the same thing, you don't have clarity—you have chaos waiting to happen.

This is not a communication exercise. It's a credibility test. A vision that can't be repeated clearly at every level is not a vision. It's a slogan.

Tool 2: The Leadership Message Matrix – Eliminating Mixed Signals

Transformation dies faster from **mixed messages** than from outright opposition. When the CEO preaches agility while the COO clings to hierarchy, employees don't resist—they freeze.

The **Leadership Message Matrix** fixes this by hardwiring alignment:

- Define 3–5 non-negotiable core messages about the transformation.
- Equip every senior leader with talking points, FAQs, and "what not to say."
- Repeat consistently, from every podium, every town hall, every memo.

When leaders speak with one voice, trust multiplies. When they don't, even the most sophisticated strategy collapses under suspicion and confusion.

Tool 3: The Culture Mapping Exercise – Exposing the DNA Misfit

Here's the lie many leaders believe: *"Culture will adapt once the strategy is clear."* Wrong. Strategy does not override culture—culture digests or rejects strategy.

The **Culture Mapping Exercise** lays this bare:

1. Identify the future behaviours required for success (e.g., speed, risk-taking, collaboration).
2. Map the current behaviours dominating the organization (e.g., hierarchy, consensus, risk-aversion).
3. Spotlight the gaps.

This is not about posters on walls. It's about confronting the invisible operating code of your organization. If you don't rewrite the code, the hardware of your transformation will keep crashing.

Tool 4: Cross-Functional SWAT Teams – Blasting Through Silos

Silos are the cholesterol of transformation. They clog the arteries of collaboration until the organization suffers a heart attack.

The antidote? **Cross-Functional SWAT Teams.**

These are not committees. They are small, empowered, diverse groups tasked with eliminating specific execution bottlenecks. They cut across functions, break turf wars, and accelerate decisions.

The hidden power of SWAT Teams isn't just problem-solving. It's relationship-building. When people from different functions work shoulder-to-shoulder, silos crumble faster than any corporate restructuring could achieve.

Tool 5: Behavioural Reinforcement Rituals – Locking Change into Daily Life

Transformation doesn't fail because people reject new behaviours. It fails because those behaviours are never reinforced long enough to become the norm.

Enter **Behavioural Reinforcement Rituals.**

- Weekly ownership shout-outs to highlight accountability.
- Daily huddles where teams recommit to their goals.
- Leaders modelling vulnerability by sharing where they fell short and what they'll do differently.

The secret is repetition. Rituals transform accountability from an initiative into identity. Without them, change withers into slogans. With them, change becomes invisible—simply "how we do things here."

Tool 6: The Transformation Impact Dashboard – Proving ROI Beyond Doubt

Transformation fatigue sets in when outcomes remain invisible. Employees ask, "What's the point?" Executives ask, "Where's the ROI?" Sceptics grow louder.

The **Transformation Impact Dashboard** answers both.

It blends:

- **Hard metrics** like revenue growth, cost savings, productivity gains, market share shifts.
- **Human signals** like engagement scores, decision-making speed, collaboration breakthroughs, and customer stories.

This dual lens ensures change is seen not just in balance sheets but in lived experience. Leaders who share this dashboard transparently—warts and all—build credibility. Those who hide the data breed cynicism.

The Reflection Discipline – Making Tools Work

Let's be clear: tools don't transform organizations. Leaders do. Tools are only as effective as the discipline with which they're applied.

So here's the real leadership challenge: **Will you use them consistently, or only when convenient?**

Ask yourself and your team, quarterly:

- Where might overconfidence be blinding us?
- Are we mistaking enthusiasm for readiness?
- Which cultural contradictions are festering beneath the surface?
- Where is communication fragmented—or absent?
- Do we have visible ROI—or are we operating on faith?
- What reinforcement mechanisms will keep this alive after the party's over?

These questions are not luxuries. They are survival checks. Ignore them, and you're gambling with millions, maybe billions, in wasted transformation spend.

From Firefighting to Future-Proofing

Most leaders still approach transformation like emergency responders. They wait for resistance, silos, or burnout to erupt, then scramble to contain the fire. By then, the damage is done.

The best leaders? They operate like architects. They design out the fires before they start. They anticipate. They prepare. They use tools that surface landmines before they detonate.

The cycle of failed transformation isn't inevitable. It's a choice. You can keep reacting—or you can start architecting.

With the **Risk Radar, Alignment Audits, Message Matrices, Culture Maps, SWAT Teams, Reinforcement Rituals, and Impact Dashboards**, you're not just equipped to manage transformation. You're equipped to lead it.

The question now is not if your transformation will face challenges. It will. The real question is: **will you be ready, or will you be surprised?**

Because in transformation, surprise is just another word for failure.

Pause and Reflect

As you close this chapter, look at your recurring transformation patterns and ask yourself:

- Which trap hit us most recently—silos, unclear decision rights, unrealistic pacing, or performative comms?
- Where are we blaming "resistance to change" instead of fixing leadership clarity?
- If we ran a **mid-execution health check** tomorrow, what truths would surface—and what would we adjust first?
- Which metric (outcome or behaviour) will we track publicly to rebuild credibility?

Next Step on the Journey

Obstacles don't vanish; they're **designed out.** Treat this chapter as your x-ray and checklist. Name the landmines, install guardrails, and create short, honest review cycles that **course-correct without blame.** With the ground made safer, your next challenge isn't launching change—it's **keeping it alive after "go-live."** That's where leaders often lose the plot and where we're headed next: **post-implementation sustainability.**

CHAPTER EIGHT

Sustaining the Flame

Making Transformation Stick After the Launch

"A leader's job is not just to inspire the destination, but to design the path, clear the roadblocks, and walk it with the team."

The Real Work Begins After "Go-Live"

The applause has faded. The banners are down. The project dashboards show "complete." For months, your organization has been immersed in a transformation—new processes, new technologies, new ways of working. Finally, you've crossed the so-called finish line.

But here's the uncomfortable truth most leaders underestimate:

Transformation is not a finish line. It's a relay race with no final baton.

Crossing the "go-live" threshold feels like an achievement – and it is. But real transformation isn't about getting to launch day. It's about what happens after the consultants leave, the training sessions end, and the initial excitement wears off.

Unfortunately, for most organizations, that's when things quietly unravel.

The Brutal Data on Post-Implementation Regression

Despite the billions spent annually on transformation programs, the majority falter within months of implementation. Consider these global findings:

- ✓ According to **McKinsey**, nearly **70% of large-scale transformations fail to sustain results beyond the first 12–18 months**, with organizations slipping back into old patterns.
- ✓ A **Bain & Company** study found that fewer than **20% of companies maintain performance improvements five years after transformation.**
- ✓ Research from **Gartner** shows that **transformation fatigue**—the slow erosion of enthusiasm and energy—affects over **60% of employees** within the first-year post-implementation.

These aren't isolated statistics—they reflect a systemic failure to plan for the long haul. The harsh reality is that most organizations celebrate "go-live" as victory, only to discover that sustainability requires a completely different set of muscles.

Why Sustainability Fails – The Hidden Landmines After Launch

The reasons transformations fade post-implementation are rarely technical. They're human, behavioural, and deeply cultural. Here's what typically happens:

1. Change Fatigue Sets In

After months (or years) of transformation effort, people are exhausted. They've sat through countless workshops, navigated system overhauls, and endured process disruptions. The collective mindset becomes:

"We've done enough. Can we please get back to normal?"

This subtle burnout breeds complacency, disengagement, and quiet resistance. Leaders misinterpret the drop in visible objections as acceptance—when it's actually apathy.

2. Regression to Old Habits

Humans are creatures of habit. Without constant reinforcement, even the most well-intentioned teams slip back into familiar, comfortable behaviors.

- Frontline employees revert to legacy workflows.
- Managers cling to old reporting structures.
- Leaders unconsciously model outdated decision-making.

It doesn't happen overnight—it's death by a thousand micro-decisions. Before long, the shiny new transformation is a distant memory.

3. Leadership Complacency Emerges

Ironically, the leaders who drive change often become its greatest risk post-implementation. The logic is understandable:

"We've invested so much energy getting here—now we can exhale."

But the moment leadership signals that change is "done," the system begins to decay. Without ongoing modelling, reinforcement, and course correction from the top, teams interpret silence as permission to revert.

In effect, leadership complacency creates cultural permission for regression.

The Myth That Kills Transformation: "Implementation = Success"

At the root of these failures is a dangerous, pervasive belief: that implementation marks the conclusion of transformation. In reality, it's just the end of the easy part—the project-based, tangible, externally visible phase.

Sustainability, on the other hand, is messier, quieter, and infinitely harder. It requires:

- Ongoing behavioural reinforcement
- Leadership self-awareness and reinvention
- Cultural maintenance rituals
- Continuous alignment between systems, behaviours, and strategy

Or as one seasoned CEO bluntly put it:

"Anyone can launch a new system. Keeping it alive when the spotlights fade? That's real leadership."

The PACE Model – Your Long-Term Sustainability Blueprint

This is where the PACE Model distinguishes itself. It wasn't designed as a flashy, one-time transformation playbook. PACE is a leadership operating system for the long haul – a practical, repeatable framework to prevent post-implementation decay.

Let's revisit how each PACE pillar reinforces sustainability:

1. Planning – But With Rolling Horizons

Sustainability requires planning that evolves. Static roadmaps become obsolete within months. PACE emphasizes **rolling plans**, quarterly recalibration, and constant strategic alignment – ensuring the organization adapts as the environment shifts.

2. Accountability – Ownership Beyond Launch

Superficial accountability evaporates after go-live. PACE embeds **dual accountability systems** – top-down clarity and bottom-up ownership – that keep leaders, teams, and individuals answerable for sustaining behaviours, not just achieving targets.

3. Communication – Sustaining Clarity and Transparency

The temptation after implementation is communication complacency. PACE instils **ongoing, transparent communication loops** – real-time feedback, decision-making clarity, and cultural storytelling – to keep alignment alive.

4. Engagement – Preventing Burnout, Building Energy

Engagement isn't a one-time initiative. PACE equips leaders with tools for **pulse engagement**, recognition-driven culture, and autonomy – preventing fatigue and keeping teams energized, even after the initial buzz fades.

In short, PACE transforms sustainability from an afterthought into an intentional, systematized practice embedded in daily leadership.

The Leadership Shift Required for Sustainability

But frameworks alone aren't enough. Sustainability depends on whether leaders themselves evolve post-implementation. Consider these mindset shifts essential for success:

Old Leadership Mindset	Sustainable Leadership Mindset
"We've arrived."	"We're iterating."
"Change was the project."	"Change is the culture."
"My role was to drive implementation."	"My role is to model ongoing growth."
"The system will sustain itself."	"The system reflects our daily behaviors."

Without these shifts, even the best-designed transformation eventually unravels.

The Silent Threat: When Sustainability Fails, It's Quiet – But Costly

The danger of post-implementation failure isn't always dramatic. It's subtle:

- Engagement quietly erodes.
- Culture slides backward.
- Talent begins to drift.
- Innovation stalls.
- Market relevance fades.

And by the time the symptoms are visible, the organization is often stuck in a costly, reactive scramble to regain momentum.

Sustainability Isn't Optional – It's the True Test of Leadership

It's easy to drive change when the spotlight is on. Real leadership is measured by what happens after the stage is dismantled, the applause fades, and the hard, quiet work of sustaining change begins.

The organizations – and leaders – who thrive post-transformation are those who understand:

"Implementation is the easy part. Keeping change alive? That's where leadership earns its stripes."

Leadership Reinvention Cycles – Staying Relevant Beyond the Transformation

Most transformation efforts begin with bold intentions – new strategies, technologies, processes, and cultural ambitions. But there's an uncomfortable reality leaders often overlook:

The greatest threat to sustaining change isn't employee resistance – it's static leadership.

You can upgrade your systems. You can overhaul your structure. You can even reshape your culture. But if leadership behaviors remain stuck in outdated patterns, the organization will quietly regress – no matter how innovative the initial transformation appeared.

True, sustainable change demands that leaders themselves evolve. This is not a one-time event. It's a continuous, intentional process known as **The Leadership Reinvention Cycle™**.

Leadership Isn't a Title – It's a Behavior That Must Evolve

Think of leadership like software. In a fast-changing world, systems that don't get updated become obsolete. The same applies to leadership:

- ✓ Markets evolve
- ✓ Technology advances
- ✓ Employee expectations shift
- ✓ Customer demands change
- ✓ Social dynamics reshape workplace culture

Yet many leaders operate with "Version 1.0" mindsets – models of authority, decision-making, and communication rooted in outdated assumptions.

The result? Even after a successful transformation, organizations experience cultural decay, loss of relevance, and a return to mediocrity.

Sustainability begins when leaders accept that reinvention is not optional – it's a professional responsibility.

The Leadership Reinvention Cycle™ – A 4-Phase Loop for Staying Relevant

Transformation collapses when leaders don't evolve as fast as the world around them. The **Leadership Reinvention Cycle™** provides a structured way to ensure leaders continuously upgrade themselves – not through sporadic retreats, but through an intentional loop of growth.

It's not linear. It's not one-off. It's a perpetual cycle that repeats as long as you hold influence.

Phase 1: Awareness – See the Gap Before It Becomes a Canyon

Reinvention begins with radical self-awareness. Leaders must identify not just *what's working*, but more importantly *what's outdated.*

- **Signals to watch**: declining team trust, missed innovation opportunities, outdated language, or feedback avoidance.
- **Tools**: 360° feedback, pulse surveys, "reverse mentoring" sessions where younger employees share insights upward.
- **Leadership Practice**: Block two hours monthly for a "mirror check" – review decisions, feedback, and market shifts. Ask: *What would my future team say I'm not ready for?*

Trap to avoid: Waiting for a crisis before confronting blind spots. By then, the gap is already a canyon.

Phase 2: Unlearning – Shedding the Baggage of Past Success

Past behaviours are like worn-out shoes: comfortable, but dangerous if you try running a new marathon in them. Leaders must deliberately **shed habits that no longer fit the new reality.**

- **Behaviours to unlearn:**
  - Equating visibility with value ("If I'm not in the room, I don't matter").
  - Command-and-control reflexes that crush autonomy.
  - Using "intuition" as a shield against data.
- **Leadership Practice**: Run a quarterly "Stop-Doing List" exercise. Write down 3 behaviours or routines you must stop because they slow down transformation. Share it with your team – and ask them to hold you accountable.

Trap to avoid: Cosmetic unlearning – leaders who *say* they've let go of old ways, but still default back under stress.

Phase 3: Relearning – Installing New Operating Software

Unlearning clears the clutter; relearning installs the upgrades. This is where leaders **acquire and embody new mindsets and capabilities.**

- **Capabilities to relearn:**
  - **Data-driven judgment**: making decisions in real time with dashboards, not quarterly hindsight.
  - **Story-driven communication**: translating strategy into narratives employees can retell.
  - **Adaptive leadership**: leading through uncertainty without rushing to control.
- **Leadership Practice:**
  - Host a "learning sprint" every 90 days – one skill you deliberately acquire or refine (e.g., AI fluency, inclusive leadership).
  - Journal weekly: *What did I try differently this week? What worked, what didn't?*

Trap to avoid: Delegating relearning to teams ("they need to get digital, not me"). If the leader doesn't embody it, the culture won't either.

Phase 4: Embedding – Making Reinvention Visible and Irreversible

Change that isn't visible isn't credible. Leaders must embed reinvention by modelling it in public and institutionalizing it in systems.

- **Embedding practices:**
  - Admit missteps openly in all-hands meetings.
  - Share "leader learnings" in newsletters or team updates.
  - Tie personal development goals into performance reviews.
- **Systemic embedding:**
  - Bake adaptability metrics into leadership scorecards.
  - Celebrate leaders who evolve, not just those who deliver results.

Trap to avoid: Treating embedding as performance theatre. Employees can spot "PR learning" from miles away. Authenticity matters more than polish.

The Loop Restarts: Renewal, Not Rest

Once embedding takes hold, the cycle doesn't end. It renews. The external environment shifts again. The team matures again. The leader must restart Awareness – spotting the next gap, the next habit to unlearn, the next skill to acquire.

The true mastery lies not in completing the cycle once but in living inside it continuously.

The **Leadership Reinvention Cycle™** is not about polishing the leader's résumé. It is about survival – for the leader and the organization. In a world where market relevance decays faster than corporate structures, leaders who cannot cycle through awareness, unlearning, relearning, and embedding simply won't last.

Reinvention isn't a choice. It's oxygen.

Behavioral Science Behind Leadership Adaptation

Leadership reinvention isn't just theory – it's rooted in behavioral science:

- **Cognitive Dissonance:** When leaders behave inconsistently with the desired culture, teams experience dissonance – and disengagement follows. Adaptation resolves this.
- **Mirror Neurons:** Neuroscience shows that humans unconsciously mimic observed behaviors. When leaders model vulnerability, curiosity, and adaptability, teams mirror those traits.
- **The Hawthorne Effect:** People modify behavior in response to observation. Leaders who consistently model evolved behaviors influence teams simply by being visible examples.
- **Neuroplasticity:** As mentioned, the brain's ability to form new neural connections enables adults – including seasoned executives – to adopt new leadership habits with deliberate practice.

In short, sustained leadership adaptation isn't just possible – it's scientifically supported.

Reflection Tool: Where Are You Stuck in the Cycle?

Leaders often get stuck at different points in the reinvention process. Use this diagnostic to identify your personal barriers:

Phase	Signal You're Stuck	Reflective Prompt
Observe	You dismiss feedback or avoid self-assessment	"What feedback am I resisting right now?"
Adapt	You recognize needed change but cling to old behaviors	"Where am I defaulting to comfort over growth?"
Embed	You change personally, but team norms stay static	"How consistently am I reinforcing new expectations?"
Elevate	You control outcomes rather than empowering others	"Where am I holding onto power that limits team growth?"

Identifying your stuck point is the first step to progress.

The Ultimate Leadership Truth: Change is a Loop, Not a Line

Sustaining transformation requires leaders to reject linear thinking. There is no final "arrival" point. Just as markets, technologies, and teams evolve – so too must leadership.

The **Leadership Reinvention Cycle™** is your practical roadmap to stay relevant, credible, and effective long after the initial transformation glow fades.

Because here's the enduring truth:

Organizations don't sustain change – leaders sustain change.

And leaders who refuse to reinvent themselves? They don't just stall progress – they become the obstacle to it.

Smart Tools for Sustaining Change

Technology as Reinforcement, Not Disruption.

When organizations hit "go-live" on transformation, the spotlight fades quickly. Leaders celebrate, consultants leave, and the company rushes back to business as usual. Yet this is when most failures occur. Not because the systems didn't work, but because the culture didn't stick.

The paradox is clear: leaders obsess about the next big technology during transformation but ignore the most powerful role tech can play **after the launch – reinforcing behaviours until they become culture.**

Technology in this phase is not about replacing people. It's about making accountability, communication, and engagement visible, repeatable, and habitual. Tools act as scaffolding until the organization is strong enough to stand on its own.

The 3 Reinforcement Functions of Technology

When used intentionally, technology sustains transformation through three essential functions:

1. Embedding Visibility

Humans trust what they can see. If progress lives only in quarterly decks, it evaporates from daily consciousness. Tech ensures that the new priorities stay on the radar.

A large retailer made conversion rate the North Star. Instead of hiding metrics in leadership dashboards, every store had a live screen showing daily progress. Teams knew instantly whether yesterday's experiments moved the needle. That visibility made performance a shared responsibility, not a top-down demand.

Visibility changes behaviour not through fear, but through transparency. People can't ignore what's right in front of them.

2. Creating Nudges

Change fails when people forget. Nudges solve this by embedding small, timely reminders into workflows.

A product development team used AI to generate meeting follow-ups. Each member received a personalized nudge the next morning: "Here's what you committed yesterday. Still on track?" These nudges turned forgotten promises into consistent follow-through.

The lesson? Nudges don't need to be fancy. They just need to show up at the right time.

3. Anchoring Rituals

The final reinforcement function is automation of cultural rituals. Rituals – like weekly retros, recognition rounds, or failure-sharing forums – turn behaviours into habits. Technology ensures they don't get skipped when urgency rises.

A pharma company running a lean transformation used its workflow system to auto-generate a short retro agenda every Friday: "What did we commit? What happened? What's next?" The system sent it to every team, ensuring the ritual survived leadership turnover and operational chaos.

Without tech, rituals rely on memory and goodwill. With tech, they become baked into the system.

The Tech Reinforcement Map

To make this concrete, here's how reinforcement technology maps directly to the PACE framework:

PACE Pillar	Reinforcement Role	Tool Application
Planning	Visibility	Live dashboards, progress trackers, heatmaps
Accountability	Nudges	AI reminders, auto-generated action lists
Communication	Anchored Rituals	Digital agendas, feedback logs, learning circles
Engagement	All Three Combined	Peer recognition platforms, storytelling hubs, cultural pulse surveys

This map reminds leaders: tech is not about shiny adoption. It's about reinforcement of the fundamentals.

1. Real-Time Performance Dashboards – Closing the Visibility Gap

Most transformations stall not because people don't want to perform, but because they can't see what matters in real time. Static quarterly reports are rear-view mirrors; leaders need dashboards that act like windshields.

- **What it solves:** Prevents blind spots, reduces rumour-driven decision-making, and creates shared focus.
- A multi-brand retailer installed real-time supply chain dashboards. Before, managers only knew about stockouts after customers complained. With the dashboards, they saw SKU-level gaps within hours and adjusted replenishment dynamically. Engagement went up because employees felt they were "winning the game with the scoreboard visible."
- **PACE link:** Dashboards strengthen *Planning* (clarity of targets) and *Accountability* (everyone knows if the ball is in their court).

2. AI-Powered Engagement Pulse Checks – Listening at Scale

Surveys taken once a year are relics. Engagement and sentiment shift weekly, sometimes daily. AI-enabled pulse checks make it possible to "put a stethoscope on organizational health" in real time.

- **What it solves:** Catches fatigue early, surfaces unspoken resistance, and helps leaders intervene before small frustrations become cultural drift.
- A pharmaceutical company used weekly AI-analysed sentiment pulses across manufacturing sites. Instead of waiting for annual survey data, leaders spotted a dip in frontline confidence after a system upgrade and quickly deployed extra training. Turnover risk dropped.
- **PACE link:** Reinforces *Engagement*, giving employees a voice and showing leaders are listening continuously.

3. Collaboration Tools That Reinforce Accountability

Technology should not just connect people – it should embed accountability into the flow of work. Modern collaboration platforms can make ownership visible, deadlines trackable, and slippage transparent.

- **What it solves:** Breaks silos, eliminates excuses, and aligns teams without relying on endless meetings.
- A fast-scaling software firm embedded accountability trackers into their project management tool. Every task showed who owned it, interdependencies, and completion risks. When a team fell behind, others could see it and offer help, instead of blaming later. This reduced firefighting by 40%.
- **PACE link:** Tightens *Accountability* by making it systemic, not personal.

Ownership is baked into the workflow.

4. Digital Storytelling Platforms for Continuous Alignment

Change dies when the story dies. Digital platforms can turn success stories, cultural wins, and leadership messages into a constant drumbeat – not a one-off town hall.

- **What it solves**: Prevents drift into old habits, reinforces purpose, and celebrates progress.
- A services firm created an internal storytelling hub where teams posted two-minute videos about customer wins tied to the transformation. Employees saw peers, not just executives, modelling new behaviours. This democratized the narrative and sustained energy months after "go-live."
- **PACE link**: Anchors *Communication*, ensuring the story stays alive long after consultants leave.

Avoiding the Over-Tech Trap

Of course, reinforcement can backfire if mishandled. Leaders often make three mistakes:

1. **Surveillance masquerading as visibility.** Dashboards that shame people erode trust. The purpose is to align, not to intimidate.
2. **Tool overload.** Every new app adds friction. If employees need six logins to update a simple metric, culture won't stick.
3. **Confusing updates with insights.** Endless reporting doesn't reinforce ownership. It buries it.

The guiding question: *Does this tool reinforce PACE?* If not, it's noise.

A Leader's Self-Check

Before implementing any reinforcement system, leaders should ask:

- **Does this tool make ownership unavoidable?**
- **Does it remind people at the moment of truth, not afterward?**
- **Does it strengthen rituals, not replace them?**
- **Does it simplify alignment, not add complexity?**

If the answer is yes, the tool is a reinforcer. If not, it's just noise dressed as innovation.

Technology won't compensate for poor leadership. But once leaders have clarified vision, modelled ownership, and created trust, technology becomes the stabilizer that holds those gains in place.

Think of tools as reinforcement beams: they don't build the house, but they keep it standing through storms.

The smartest leaders don't ask, *"What's the next platform we should buy?"* They ask, *"How do we use tools to make accountability visible, communication consistent, engagement habitual, and planning transparent?"*

In the end, sustainability isn't luck. It's leadership reinforced – one dashboard, one nudge, one ritual at a time.

Tech is the Amplifier – Leadership is the Foundation

In the rush to sustain transformation, it's tempting to rely on platforms, apps, and dashboards as the solution. But the truth is simpler – and more demanding:

Technology sustains nothing if leadership behaviors decay.

The organizations that sustain change long-term:

- ✓ Invest in tools that increase visibility, connection, and alignment
- ✓ Ensure leaders are visible, consistent, and accountable within those tools
- ✓ Use technology to enhance, not automate, cultural reinforcement

Technology-Augmented Leadership isn't about replacing human connection – it's about scaling it.

Because in the end, the tools you deploy are only as powerful as the leadership that guides them.

Measuring Transformation Success – The PACE-Based KPI System

Most organizations measure success the moment a transformation goes "live."

Revenue uptick? Check.

Efficiency gains? Check.

Employee satisfaction bump? Check.

But here's the harsh truth:

Short-term wins are seductive – and dangerously misleading.

Many organizations declare victory too early, celebrating visible but temporary improvements while the deeper roots of transformation remain weak. Within 12–24 months, the old behaviors creep back, engagement drops, silos reappear, and performance plateaus – or worse, declines.

Sustainable transformation demands sustained measurement.

But not the outdated, lagging, surface-level metrics many leaders default to.

Instead, leaders must adopt a **PACE-Based KPI System** – a practical, predictive framework that tracks the real signals of long-term success: behavior change, cultural reinforcement, and system alignment.

The Danger of Measuring the Wrong Things

The graveyard of failed transformations is filled with organizations that:

- ✓ Measured activity, not ownership
- ✓ Focused on outputs, not behaviors
- ✓ Chased short-term performance at the expense of culture
- ✓ Ignored early signals of disengagement and regression

It's like declaring a weight loss program successful after one week on the scale – ignoring diet, habits, and long-term health.

Transformation is no different. Leaders need to measure what truly sustains change – even if it's harder, more subjective, and less glamorous than simple output numbers.

Introducing the PACE Sustainability KPI Framework

The **PACE-Based KPI System** is designed for exactly this challenge. It goes beyond traditional performance metrics to track the health, integrity, and endurance of transformation across the four pillars of PACE:

- Planning
- Accountability
- Communication
- Engagement

These aren't theoretical ideals – they're measurable, observable drivers of transformation sustainability.

Let's break them down.

Planning: Measuring Adaptive Discipline

Sustainable organizations don't treat planning as a static, annual exercise. They treat it as a living discipline – a rhythm of constant review and recalibration. The strongest signal of adaptive discipline is how frequently leaders revisit and revise their strategies. Quarterly reviews are no longer a luxury; they're a necessity. When those reviews surface fresh market data, cultural signals, and operational insights, leaders have the chance to reset direction before drift turns into derailment.

Equally telling is whether teams themselves have documented plans that line up with the broader organizational direction. If only executives can describe the strategy, the transformation will fracture across departments. Another key indicator of resilience is the speed at which plans are adjusted after disruption. Markets move quickly. A six-month lag between shock and response is no longer acceptable.

Finally, planning must be inclusive. If frontline voices are absent, leaders risk designing in an echo chamber. Cross-functional participation is not just nice to have – it's the test of whether planning is grounded in reality.

The warning signs are clear: plans that gather dust, responses that lag behind market conditions, and strategies confined to the top tier. These are not evidence of discipline but symptoms of fragility.

Accountability: Measuring Ownership, Not Just Compliance

True accountability is not about punishment. It's about creating a system where ownership is felt, shared, and reinforced. One way to test if accountability is alive is to ask whether peers hold each other to commitments – not just whether managers chase deadlines. Peer-to-peer accountability scores, tracked through 360-degree feedback, reveal whether teams truly own outcomes together.

Another strong measure is clarity. If team members cannot articulate their role in the transformation in simple terms, accountability hasn't been established – it's just been delegated. Organizations that track resolution rates for missed commitments, and measure whether follow-through happens within agreed timelines, create a culture where accountability becomes muscle memory rather than managerial enforcement.

Pulse surveys also expose how consistently managers follow through on promises. When leaders fail to close the loop, accountability collapses into finger-pointing.

The red flags here are obvious: accountability that flows only top-down, a culture of excuses, and missed commitments tolerated in silence. These patterns don't reflect ownership – they reflect avoidance.

Communication: Measuring Clarity and Feedback Health

Change dies not from lack of information but from lack of clarity. Sustainable communication is not about volume; it is about precision and feedback. Organizations that thrive in transformation measure their "clarity score" – whether employees understand what is changing, why it matters, and how it affects them. If the message doesn't land at the frontline, it never truly existed.

Another crucial measure is the speed at which feedback loops close. If employees raise concerns and those concerns vanish into a void, mistrust festers. On the other hand, when issues are acknowledged and acted on quickly, communication shifts from theatre to trust-building.

Effective organizations also monitor whether employees consistently receive transparent updates, not just during launch periods but throughout the transformation journey. The health of a cascade can be tested: if frontline employees can repeat the key priorities in their own words, the system is working. If they can't, it's noise.

Red flags are equally clear: an overload of generic corporate announcements, feedback channels that operate like black holes, and frontline confusion about strategy. These aren't just communication failures – they're signals that transformation is slipping out of alignment.

Engagement: Measuring Energy and Emotional Connection

Engagement is not satisfaction. It is energy, ownership, and the emotional connection people feel to the mission. One of the strongest indicators is an "energy pulse score," measured monthly. When energy dips, burnout or disengagement is often just below the surface.

Recognition is another powerful proxy. Sustainable organizations track how often formal and informal recognition happens. If people's ownership behaviours aren't being noticed, accountability begins to feel like drudgery. Teams that track psychological safety ratings also have a window into whether people feel safe to experiment, challenge, and innovate – the true drivers of long-term engagement.

Attrition tells its own story. Voluntary departures of high performers are not just HR issues; they are strategic alarms. When top talent exits, it signals disengagement at the deepest level.

The warning signs are unmistakable: engagement measured only once a year, superficial perks masquerading as culture, and burnout or quiet quitting dismissed as anomalies. These are not small cracks – they are structural failures in the emotional infrastructure of transformation.

PACE Sustainability in Action

A practical **PACE Sustainability Scorecard** might look like this:

PACE Pillar	Key KPI	Target	Current	Trend
Planning	Strategic Review Cycle Frequency	Quarterly	On Track	↑
Accountability	Peer Ownership Score	80%+	72%	↓
Communication	Feedback Loop Closure Time	< 7 days	9 days	↓
Engagement	Employee Energy Pulse	75%+	68%	↓

Leadership Insight:
This organization has solid planning discipline but slipping accountability, slower feedback loops, and declining engagement – early warning signs of regression.

The scorecard doesn't just report – it informs where to intervene.

Are You Measuring What Actually Sustains Change?

Pause and reflect:

- Are your KPIs tracking short-term activity or long-term behavior?
- How often are you measuring employee energy, ownership, and alignment?
- Can your frontline teams articulate their role in sustaining change?
- Are your scorecards highlighting cultural health – or just financial outputs?

If the answer to any of these is "no," you may be flying blind into the post-transformation danger zone.

The Bottom Line: Metrics Aren't Just for Compliance – They're for Course Correction

Sustaining transformation isn't about luck or hope – it's about disciplined measurement, continuous learning, and courageous intervention.

The **PACE-Based KPI System** provides the roadmap:

✓ **Planning** – Stay adaptable, aligned, and responsive
✓ **Accountability** – Track ownership, not just tasks
✓ **Communication** – Measure clarity and feedback health
✓ **Engagement** – Monitor energy, recognition, and connection

The organizations that thrive post-transformation aren't perfect – but they're relentlessly curious, data-informed, and willing to confront hard truths.

Because what gets measured gets sustained – but only if you're measuring what truly matters.

Sustaining Your Legacy Through PACE

Transformation is never a single moment of triumph. It's a discipline. A rhythm.

A way of leading that refuses to let change fade into memory.

You've seen the hard truth:

- ✓ Most transformations stall not in the launch phase, but in the quiet months and years that follow.
- ✓ Culture, accountability, engagement—they either grow stronger over time or quietly erode.
- ✓ Leaders themselves are often the biggest variable in sustaining—or sabotaging—the gains.

The real question isn't, "Did you implement change?"
The real question is, **"Did you embed it so deeply that it outlives you?"**

That is the true test of leadership legacy.

PACE: More Than a Model – It's a Legacy Blueprint

The PACE model—**Planning, Accountability, Communication, Engagement**—was never designed as a quick-fix framework. It's a long-game system that helps leaders do three critical things over time:

1. **Reinforce what matters, relentlessly.**
2. **Adapt to evolving challenges without losing cultural coherence.**
3. **Transfer ownership of success to the entire organization, not just the top team.**

When PACE becomes woven into your daily leadership rhythms—when it shifts from being an initiative to becoming invisible muscle memory—**that's when transformation sticks.**

And that's when your legacy starts to compound.

The Difference Between Change That Fades and Change That Lasts

Short-lived change is seductive. It's often sparked by a charismatic leader, a big kick-off event, or an inspiring town hall. For a while, the energy feels unstoppable. But because it rests on personalities rather than systems, and because it is measured by short-term wins alone, the momentum quickly fizzles. Once attention shifts elsewhere, the initiative loses oxygen. What remains is a trail of forgotten slogans, half-adopted processes, and employees who quietly slip back into old ways of working.

Sustained change looks very different. It isn't built on one person's energy but on institutional discipline. Planning cycles are clear and adaptive, ensuring the organization course-corrects when reality shifts. Accountability runs across all levels, not just top-down, so ownership becomes a shared practice. Communication remains transparent and timely, helping people see progress and trust leadership even during setbacks. And engagement is not staged or performative; it is embedded into everyday rituals, creating an authentic sense of belonging and purpose.

The organizations that continue to thrive long after the banners come down aren't the ones with the flashiest launches. They are the ones where leaders keep showing up – curious enough to ask questions, humble enough to admit missteps, and consistent enough to reinforce new behaviours until they become second nature. In these organizations, PACE isn't a program or a framework on paper. It becomes the cultural operating system – quiet, steady, and enduring.

The Hardest Truth: Your Legacy Isn't Defined by the Launch

It's defined by:

✓ How you evolve when the cameras are off
✓ How rigorously you measure what matters
✓ How visibly you model growth and accountability
✓ How empowered your teams feel to sustain the momentum without you

Anyone can drive short-term change. But few leaders have the discipline, humility, and systems to sustain it.

Pause and Reflect

As you close this chapter, look at how results are sustained after rollout and ask yourself:

- What will make the change still visible 90 days after "complete"–in dashboards and daily behaviors?

- Which two reinforcement rituals (reviews, recognition, pulse responses) will we commit to weekly?
- Where might regression occur—and what early warning signal will we watch?
- Which one leader (besides me) will become a culture carrier for this?

Next Step on the Journey

Sustainability is the quiet hero of transformation: **small, reliable signals** that say "this is how we work now." When measurement meets meaning, teams keep rowing after the banners come down. With your flywheel turning, it's time to look outward: the next horizon of leadership, where AI and emerging tech change speed and scale—yet the human operating system of PACE must remain intact.

CHAPTER NINE

The Next Horizon of Leadership

Human-Centered Mastery in an AI-Driven World

"Technology can build faster, but only leadership can build trust. Tools may shape the future of work – principles will shape the future of leadership."

The Disruption Dilemma

"Buildings don't stand because of hammers. They stand because of physics. Leadership is the same: tools evolve—integrity doesn't."

In every generation, leadership faces a reckoning. A moment when tools evolve so dramatically that old models begin to crack. The steam engine forced leaders of the Industrial Revolution to rethink how they organized labour. The arrival of global trade routes forced leaders to rethink supply chains and governance. The rise of digital technology forced leaders to rethink communication, decision-making, and customer engagement.

We are living through another such moment now – one fuelled by **artificial intelligence, blockchain, automation, and exponential change.** The speed, scale, and scope of disruption is unlike anything leaders have faced before.

The temptation, as always, is to cling to familiar playbooks. To believe that what worked yesterday can be stretched into tomorrow. To tell ourselves that a few tweaks will suffice. But history shows otherwise: **when the tools change exponentially, the leadership operating system must be rewritten.**

The Illusion of Control

Disruption is not polite. It doesn't knock on the door and wait to be invited in. It barges through the walls.

In a decentralized world powered by blockchain and distributed systems, leaders who cling to centralization face a rude awakening. In an AI-driven world where algorithms can generate strategy options in seconds, leaders who rely on slow consensus risk irrelevance.

The illusion of control is seductive. Dashboards give us the sense that we are watching everything. Automation gives us the sense that systems are self-correcting. But visibility is not control. Logs are not ownership. Tools are not leadership.

Provocative question: *If your organization lost all its dashboards tomorrow, would your people still know what to do?*

Why Old Models Fail Under Exponential Tech

Most leaders don't fail because they lack intelligence. They fail because they misapply outdated models to a new reality.

Three failure patterns dominate:

1. **Confusing tools with principles.** Leaders assume AI equals foresight, blockchain equals trust, automation equals ownership. But principles cannot be automated. Without human intent, technology magnifies dysfunction instead of eliminating it.
2. **Collapsing under speed.** Traditional models assume you can deliberate endlessly, build consensus slowly, and adapt at leisure. But exponential technology moves faster than human committees. By the time you finish debating, the world has moved on.
3. **Ignoring the human core.** Algorithms may optimize processes, but people resist when they don't see meaning. A dashboard can flag declining morale, but it cannot make employees feel seen, valued, or inspired.

This is why studies consistently show 70% of digital transformation initiatives fall short of expectations. Not because the tools are flawed, but because leadership systems are.

The Old vs. The New

Old Model	Why It Fails	PACE Upgrade
Static planning cycles – annual budgets, five-year roadmaps	Collapse under constant disruption; irrelevant by the time they are published	**Planning** as rolling, scenario-based portfolios reviewed weekly
Top-down accountability – leaders delegate, teams comply	Creates compliance but not ownership; people wait to be told	**Accountability** built on radical clarity and shared responsibility
One-way communication – memos, reports, endless meetings	Slow, tone-deaf, and often irrelevant	**Communication** that is contextual, multi-channel, emotionally intelligent
Engagement as perks – bonuses, Friday pizza, superficial recognition	Short-lived enthusiasm; doesn't create meaning	**Engagement** rooted in belonging, purpose, and human connection

This table is not theory. It is the daily reality of organizations stuck between old systems and new expectations.

The Planning Failure

One local organization rolled out an ambitious AI-powered forecasting tool. Executives believed it would solve their planning woes. The system generated dozens of projections, each more detailed than the last. But leadership still clung to the old model of **annual planning.** They treated AI outputs as fixed predictions rather than living scenarios.

By midyear, conditions had shifted dramatically. Demand projections were wrong, but budgets were locked. Teams were demoralized. People whispered: *"Why do we even bother with forecasts if we're not allowed to change course?"*

The tool wasn't the problem. The **planning model was.** Had leadership used – rolling reviews, assumption logs, and adaptive prioritization – the technology could have amplified foresight. Instead, it amplified rigidity.

If AI and Blockchain Change the *How*, PACE Defines the *What*

This is the disruption dilemma: technology keeps changing the **how** of leadership, but it never redefines the **what.**

- **Planning** remains about focusing finite attention on the vital few priorities, no matter how many simulations AI can run.
- **Accountability** remains about turning intentions into ownership, no matter how many ledgers track transactions.
- **Communication** remains about clarity and trust, no matter how many platforms generate summaries.
- **Engagement** remains about inspiring meaning, no matter how many surveys pulse sentiment.

Technology is your **power tool.** PACE is your **blueprint.** One without the other builds nothing of value.

Diagnostic: Is Your Leadership Model Expiring?

Here's a quick litmus test. Answer honestly:

- Do you have more than five "top priorities" at any given time?
- Do actions often lack clear owners and deadlines?
- Do meetings end without decisions captured in a single sentence?
- Do AI pilots exist without adoption criteria or go/no-go metrics?
- Do fewer than 70% of employees respond to engagement surveys?
- Do escalations take more than 24 hours to reach the right owner?

If you answered "yes" to three or more, your leadership model is expiring.

The Communication Breakdown

A fast-growing firm adopted a suite of collaboration tools. Messages flew across multiple platforms: emails, chats, shared dashboards. Leaders assumed that **more communication channels meant better communication.**

Instead, noise exploded. Critical updates were buried. Employees stopped checking dashboards. Escalations were delayed because no one knew which channel mattered most.

When surveyed, 62% of employees said: *"I spend more time figuring out where to look than doing my job."*

The tools were not the problem. The absence of a **communication framework** was. PACE would have solved it through a **Communication Heatmap**: defining audience, purpose, channel, cadence, and ownership for every message stream.

From Threat to Opportunity

The fear is misplaced. Technology is not the enemy of leadership. It is the test of leadership. It asks:

- Can you adapt faster than disruption?
- Can you ground new tools in timeless principles?
- Can you inspire people to trust in a future that feels uncertain?

Future-ready leaders don't resist tools – they **orchestrate them through PACE.** They don't confuse dashboards with decisions, logs with ownership, or metrics with meaning. They know that tools multiply what already exists. If you lead poorly, AI will scale dysfunction. If you lead with PACE, AI will magnify impact.

Leader Moves

- **Name your vital few.** Limit top priorities to 3–5 and publish them.
- **Close the loop in meetings.** Every action has an owner and deadline spoken aloud.
- **Document decisions in one sentence.** Share within 15 minutes of meeting close.
- **Define adoption criteria for AI pilots.** No rollout without clear go/no-go thresholds.
- **Run a five-question weekly pulse.** Commit to responding within 72 hours.

The disruption dilemma is not whether tools will change leadership. They already have. The real dilemma is whether you will cling to expired models or evolve through PACE.

Outdated leadership models expire. PACE endures.

The Augmented Leader – Technology Serves, Humanity Leads

"AI is the calculator. You're still doing the thinking."

Every leap in human history has carried the same fear: *"Will this tool replace us?"*

- When the abacus appeared, scribes feared their skills would vanish.
- When the steam engine emerged, craftsmen feared machines would erase artisanship.
- When spreadsheets arrived, finance teams feared redundancy.

The answer, every time, was the same: tools replaced labour, not leadership.

Today, AI, blockchain, and automation spark the same panic. Yet technology does not replace judgment, empathy, or moral courage. It amplifies them—or exposes their absence.

The future-ready leader is not the one who hands decisions to machines, but the one who integrates machines into **PACE**—ensuring technology serves, while humanity leads.

The Myth of the Tool-Driven Leader

Just because you have AI dashboards doesn't mean you have clarity. Just because you use blockchain doesn't mean you have trust. Just because you automate workflows doesn't mean you have accountability.

Technology is not leadership. It is a **multiplier**: of clarity or confusion, ownership or excuses, belonging or alienation.

Provocative question: *If AI multiplied your leadership tenfold tomorrow, would your people thank you—or leave you?*

PACE Pillars in a Tech World

Let's examine each pillar under the pressure of technology. Each reveals the same truth: tools can augment, but they cannot replace.

1. Planning: Models Inform, Leaders Decide

Myth: AI makes planning automatic.
Truth: AI can generate thousands of scenarios, but leaders must still choose purpose, priorities, and trade-offs.

AI might forecast supply chain disruptions, optimize workforce schedules, or predict customer demand. But it cannot decide which markets to enter, which risks to embrace, or which bets align with purpose. That is the leader's domain.

Leader Moves

- Run **three-option scenarios** (best/base/worst) and decide deliberately.
- Hold a **weekly Choices Forum**: 30 minutes to review AI insights and confirm priorities.
- Publish an **assumption log**: list what each plan depends on, and update as facts evolve.

One logistics company relied on AI forecasts to set quarterly plans. The forecasts were precise, but leadership treated them as guarantees. When geopolitical shocks hit, the model collapsed – and so did confidence. What failed? Not the AI, but leadership's refusal to adapt. Had they used PACE's rolling Planning, they would have course-corrected faster.

2. Accountability: Logs Record, Humans Own

Myth: Blockchain ensures accountability.
Truth: Ledgers record tasks; only leaders create ownership.

Technology can prove that a promise was made. It cannot make anyone care enough to deliver. Accountability without ownership is bureaucracy in disguise.

Leader Moves

- Apply the **Accountability Ladder**: coach people from "I'll try" → "I own it."
- End every meeting with owners stating deadlines aloud. Social commitment drives follow-through.
- Circulate a **visual action board** within 15 minutes after each meeting.

One leading firm piloted an AI tool to rank job candidates. The system produced biased outcomes. Instead of hiding behind the algorithm, leadership created a cross-functional **Ethics Council**. They reclaimed **Accountability** by declaring: *"The AI assists, but we own the decision."* Trust rose, not because the tool improved, but because ownership was visible.

If your systems record every task but no one owns the outcome, is that accountability—or just organized failure?

3. Communication: AI Drafts, Leaders Inspire

Myth: Generative AI ensures clarity.
Truth: AI can draft memos, but clarity without trust is noise.

AI may reduce clutter, but tone, empathy, and credibility remain human. A flawless summary delivered without care still leaves people cold.

Leader Moves

- Build a **Communication Heatmap**: map audience, purpose, channel, cadence.
- Cap updates at **five bullets** plus one headline decision.
- Define and publish **escalation rules**: who, when, how.

A professional services firm deployed AI to condense reports. Leaders stopped contextualizing the summaries. Employees said: *"The updates are faster, but they feel soulless."* When leaders reintroduced personal framing – explaining *why* each decision mattered – trust returned.

If AI speaks perfectly but without empathy, who will your people choose to follow – the system or you?

4. Engagement: Platforms Measure, Leaders Connect

Myth: Engagement platforms drive motivation.
Truth: Tools measure sentiment; leaders create belonging.

Dashboards can show declining morale. They cannot inspire meaning. Pulse surveys can highlight burnout, but without a leader's response, data becomes demoralization.

Leader Moves

- Run a **weekly five-question pulse** and respond within 72 hours.
- Make **daily recognition rituals** non-negotiable.
- Rotate **voice rounds**: everyone speaks once before meetings close.

A tech-enabled factory installed sensors to measure team fatigue. Data showed exhaustion rising, but nothing changed. Morale sank further. When leaders stepped in – co-creating rest breaks, acknowledging strain, and adjusting workloads – engagement rebounded. The platform didn't drive connection. People did.

When Tech Fails, Leadership Intervenes

Technology doesn't fail because of what it can do; it fails because of how leaders apply it.

Failure Mode	PACE Intervention	What Changes Next Week
Pilot purgatory	**Planning**: set scale criteria; **Accountability**: assign owners	A go/no-go forum booked; criteria visible
Data disputes	**Communication**: agree one dashboard; set escalation path	Single version of truth; disputes resolved in 24h
Tool fatigue	**Engagement**: run a stop–start audit	Two low-value rituals cut; team energy restored
Shadow ownership	**Accountability**: visible action board	90% of tasks tied to owners with dates

People-First AI

A manufacturer deployed AI vision systems for defect detection. The algorithm worked, but operators felt blamed when false positives spiked. Rework rose; overtime costs ballooned.

Leaders reset through PACE. **Planning** narrowed scope to three defect types. **Accountability** shifted sign-off to line owners. **Communication** shifted to 10-minute huddles with one screen, one decision. **Engagement** came from weekly operator feedback loops retraining the model.

Within weeks, false positives fell 42%, first-pass yield rose six points, and overtime shrank. The AI didn't change. Leadership did.

The Augmented Leader's Mindset

The augmented leader views technology as an ally, not a rival. They:

- Let AI inform judgment, never replace it.
- Demand ownership, not just records.
- Deliver meaning, not just summaries.
- Translate sentiment into belonging.

Technology is powerful. But power without principle is chaos. **PACE ensures power serves purpose.**

Leader Moves

- Hold a **weekly Choices Forum**: choose, don't just debate.
- Close meetings with **spoken deadlines** and a shared action board photo.
- Deliver updates capped at **five bullets** with one decision headline.
- Enforce a **72-hour pulse-response rule**: never let sentiment sit idle.
- Celebrate one **micro-win per day** to sustain energy.

Technology serves. Humanity leads. **PACE ensures it stays that way.**

Human-Centric Leadership

"Machines may outperform us in speed – but not in meaning."

Technology promises efficiency, scale, and predictive power. Yet with each new adoption, leaders face a paradox: the more we automate, the more alienated people often feel.

Dashboards expose gaps but seldom explain purpose. AI tools accelerate decisions but rarely address emotions. Surveys capture sentiment but often fail to spark action. The result? **A trust deficit** – people are surrounded by data but starved of meaning.

The organizations that thrive will not be those with the flashiest platforms, but those with leaders who understand a profound truth: **technology may enable**

performance, but humanity sustains it.

The Trust Deficit in Tech-Led Systems

A 2024 industry survey found that more than 60% of employees in tech-centric workplaces reported feeling *less connected to leadership.* Not because tools malfunctioned, but because the human voice behind them went silent.

This trust deficit emerges in three fractures:

1. **Speed vs. Comprehension**
   Technology accelerates output, but people cannot process meaning at machine speed. Leaders must pause to explain *why* decisions matter.
2. **Transparency vs. Care**
   Dashboards reveal everything, but without empathetic framing, they feel like surveillance. Transparency without care creates fear, not trust.
3. **Monitoring vs. Belonging**
   Pulse surveys collect feedback, but if leaders fail to respond, employees disengage. Measurement without follow-through erodes connection.

Provocative question: *If your team feels monitored but not mentored, are they truly engaged – or just observed?*

The Human Operating System of PACE

Technology may change workflows, but **PACE anchors the human OS** that technology cannot replicate.

- **Planning with People, Not Just Data**
  AI can model scenarios, but only people closest to the work can highlight hidden risks and practical trade-offs. Inclusive planning builds ownership.
- **Accountability with Grace, Not Just Logs**
  Blockchain may track actions, but leaders must distinguish between effort mistakes and intent failures. Coaching, not punishment, builds accountability.
- **Communication with Care, Not Just Clarity**
  AI can condense messages, but leaders must add empathy, context, and tone. People follow meaning, not just information.
- **Engagement with Belonging, Not Just Feedback Loops**

Platforms can measure morale, but leaders must create belonging through recognition, inclusion, and purpose.

The Hybrid Reset

One global organization adopted AI-driven scheduling and collaboration tools to enable hybrid work. Productivity metrics looked impressive, but trust plummeted. Employees felt micromanaged by algorithms and disconnected from leaders.

PACE provided the reset.

- **Planning with people:** Teams co-created weekly priorities with managers.
- **Accountability with grace:** Missed deadlines triggered learning reviews, not blame.
- **Communication with care:** Updates became shorter, contextual, and empathetic.
- **Engagement with belonging:** Leaders held monthly listening rounds with no slides, just open questions.

Within three months, attrition fell, engagement scores rose, and productivity stabilized at higher levels. The tools didn't change – leadership did.

The Trust Stack

Trust doesn't emerge automatically. It is built deliberately, layer by layer, like a stack. Miss one, and the structure collapses.

1. **Transparency** – People see how decisions are made.
2. **Consent** – They know where they can influence outcomes.
3. **Oversight** – They understand how AI and tools are monitored.
4. **Redress** – They have safe avenues to raise concerns and seek correction.

A transparent dashboard without oversight breeds fear. Consent without redress creates cynicism. Only when all four layers exist does trust in technology become real.

Provocative question: *If your systems are transparent but people feel powerless to shape them, is that trust – or exposure?*

Purpose-Led Planning

Another organization, known for its values-driven culture, faced rising collaboration fatigue as global teams scaled. Tools multiplied, but meaning thinned.

Leaders doubled down on humanity:

- **Planning with people:** Frontline employees co-authored priorities.
- **Accountability with grace:** Missed goals were reviewed for lessons, not punishment.
- **Communication with care:** Every update tied metrics back to shared purpose.
- **Engagement with belonging:** Company-wide calls ended with individuals sharing how their week's work connected to values.

The result? Productivity rose, but more importantly, employees reported *higher meaning and belonging scores* than before the tech expansion. Technology scaled operations. Leadership preserved the soul.

Why Humanity Becomes the Edge

Competitors can copy your platforms. They can license the same AI or purchase the same dashboards. But they cannot replicate the trust, belonging, and loyalty your people feel when leadership shows genuine care.

Machines may outperform humans in speed, scale, and precision. But they cannot:

- Create shared purpose.
- Build cultures of accountability.
- Deliver empathy in difficult conversations.
- Inspire commitment in the face of uncertainty.

In other words, the **last competitive moat is not technology – it is humanity.**

Leader Moves

- **Run co-creation workshops** for setting priorities: ask *"What do you see that I don't?"*
- **Coach accountability**: use the Accountability Ladder to develop ownership instead of punishing misses.

- **Default to public summaries.** Keep updates visible unless privacy is required.
- **Apply a 72-hour response rule** for engagement surveys: never let feedback sit idle.
- **Host monthly listening rounds:** no slides, just leader presence.

Engagement Beyond Metrics

A services company installed continuous engagement dashboards. Leaders assumed constant data would guarantee morale. Instead, employees felt like lab subjects. *"We are being measured, not heard,"* one employee said.

When leaders shifted gears, things changed. They **acted visibly on survey results** within 72 hours, celebrated micro-wins daily, and invited team stories about purpose during town halls. Suddenly, the same tool became a trust-builder – because leaders closed the loop.

Technology is neutral. It can either widen disconnection or deepen belonging, depending on how leaders use it.

Machines may outperform us in speed – but not in meaning. The organizations that endure will be those where leaders lean into humanity. **PACE is the blueprint that ensures you never lose it.**

Future-Proofing the PACE Framework

"Technology is your power tool. PACE is your blueprint. One without the other builds nothing of value."

Strategy cycles that once spanned five years are now compressed into five months. Platforms that dazzled last quarter are obsolete today. AI models that seemed cutting-edge yesterday are surpassed before teams even finish implementation. Leaders are tempted to believe the next platform or algorithm will finally "solve" execution.

But tools, however powerful, remain powerless without principles. They cannot substitute for the timeless physics of leadership: clarity, ownership, trust, and belonging.

This is where **PACE 2.0** enters – not as a replacement, but as an **evolution.** The principles endure; the practices adapt. The blueprint remains; the power tools change.

From Yesterday to Tomorrow: The Shift

PACE 2.0 acknowledges that the environment is radically different. Linear strategy is dead. Ownership is no longer confined to hierarchical charts. Communication is no longer one-way or static. Engagement cannot be reduced to quarterly surveys.

Pillar	Yesterday	PACE 2.0 Upgrade	Leader Ritual
Planning	Annual plans + firefighting	Scenario portfolios with rolling reviews	Weekly 30-min "Choices Forum"
Accountability	Task lists in tools	Ownership ledgers + Accountability Ladder coaching	Spoken deadlines + photo of action board
Communication	Email floods + meeting overload	Communication Heatmaps + AI summaries	Five-bullet updates + decision headline
Engagement	Quarterly HR surveys	Continuous five-question pulses + human follow-through	72-hour response rule + daily micro-wins

This is not theory. These are the shifts leaders must embody if they want their organizations to remain resilient under exponential disruption.

Why PACE 2.0 Matters Now

Consider this:

- AI accelerates decisions, but without **Planning**, you scale chaos.
- Blockchain logs commitments, but without **Accountability**, you log excuses.
- Generative AI writes memos, but without **Communication**, you distribute sterile noise.
- Engagement dashboards collect data, but without **human follow-through**, you automate disappointment.

Technology magnifies what already exists. If dysfunction rules, tools will scale dysfunction. If discipline rules, tools will scale discipline. **PACE is the governor of** that equation.

The Meeting Reset

A global enterprise implemented AI-assisted scheduling and workflow systems. Meetings multiplied instead of shrinking. Leaders drowned in noise.

PACE 2.0 intervened. Meetings were forced into a **no-decision, no-meeting** rule. A weekly **Choices Forum** replaced ad-hoc debates. Decisions were captured in five-bullet updates with one headline. Suddenly, the same tools became enablers rather than burdens.

Lesson: technology didn't simplify the system. Leadership discipline did.

The Non-Negotiables of PACE 2.0

Future-proofing requires discipline. Leaders cannot cherry-pick principles when convenient. PACE 2.0 comes with four **non-negotiables**:

1. **No initiative without an owner and a date.**
   Every project must have a name and a deadline attached. Without this, execution dissolves into wish lists.
2. **No meeting without a decision or a kill.**
   If nothing is decided, the meeting was noise. Either progress or closure — but never drift.
3. **No pulse without a response.**
   If you ask for feedback, you must close the loop within 72 hours. Silence destroys trust faster than bad news.
4. **No technology rollout without a PACE adoption plan.**
   A new tool must be anchored in Planning, Accountability, Communication, and Engagement. Otherwise, it becomes theatre.

These are simple. That is the point. Complexity collapses under pressure; principles endure.

Leader Moves: Future-Proofing in Practice

- **Choices Forum:** Every week, leaders review three scenarios and select one, publishing rationale.
- **Action Board Ritual:** Photograph commitments at meeting close and

share with the team within 15 minutes.

- **Communication Heatmap:** Map out who needs what, when, and in what channel.
- **Pulse Rhythm:** Run a five-question pulse every week and publish responses within three days.
- **Micro-Win Celebrations: End each shift or meeting with a recognition tied to purpose.**

When practiced consistently, these moves shift organizations from reactive to resilient.

The Engagement Failure

A services company launched a high-tech engagement platform that pulsed employees every week. Participation soared at first, but quickly collapsed. Employees said: *"Why bother? Nothing changes."*

Leaders enforced the **72-hour feedback response rule.** Every survey result was acknowledged, actioned, or explained within three days. Engagement not only recovered – it exceeded initial levels. People realized feedback wasn't disappearing into the void.

Lesson: platforms don't engage people. **Follow-through does.**

Reasserting the Leader's Role

- Technology may inform decisions, but leaders must still choose.
- Technology may log commitments, but leaders must still build ownership.
- Technology may summarize messages, but leaders must still deliver meaning.
- Technology may measure mood, but leaders must still create belonging.

PACE 2.0 does not reduce the leader's role – it magnifies it. It reminds leaders that while tools evolve, **their authority comes from clarity, courage, and care.**

Pause and Reflect

As you close this chapter, look at how technology is amplifying—not replacing—leadership in your organization and ask yourself:

- Where will tech be our power tool—and where must leadership remain the blueprint?
- Which decision this month will we make with AI input but by human judgment—and how will we explain it?
- What new cadence (spoken deadlines, five-bullet decisions, rapid pulse responses) will we adopt to keep speed with integrity?
- Which skill will I coach in my team to raise our human advantage (sense-making, trust-building, narrative clarity)?

Next Step on the Journey

Tools upgrade the hardware; **PACE is the operating system.** Anchor in principles, then amplify with technology. Choose one PACE 2.0 upgrade and run it for 30 days—measure decision speed, action closure, and sentiment. As you step into the final chapter, remember: the ultimate test of leadership is not a launch; it's a **legacy**. We now move from framework to **flame**—from practiced routines to a culture that outlives its authors.

CHAPTER TEN

From Framework to Flame

Embedding PACE as a Living Culture

"Frameworks guide leaders. Flames inspire legacies. Your task is not to manage the spark, but to keep the fire alive."

From Framework to Living Practice

Every framework begins as an idea. A model sketched on a whiteboard. A playbook tucked into leadership decks. But ideas don't transform organizations – behaviours do. And behaviours become culture only when they are lived, not preached.

PACE was never meant to stay as a four-letter acronym in binders. It was designed to be practiced until it breathes through every corridor of the organization – not as an initiative, but as a way of life. That is the difference between a framework and a flame. A framework can instruct; a flame can inspire, illuminate, and endure.

The Risk of Framework Fatigue

Most organizations don't fail for lack of models. They fail because those models never leave the slide deck. A consulting framework arrives with great fanfare, leaders champion it for a season, and then... silence. The energy fades, the rituals disappear, and the organization drifts back into old habits.

This is **framework fatigue**: when people grow tired of new acronyms and promises that never make it into their daily work. Leaders must guard against this. Because when PACE is treated as another passing management fad, it loses its power.

PACE must outlive the "program of the year." It must become the unseen hand that guides every decision, conversation, and behaviour.

PACE as Muscle, Not Memory

Think of PACE as a muscle. Reading about it once is like watching a workout video – you may understand the moves, but nothing changes in your body. Strength comes only from repetition, resistance, and persistence.

- **Planning** becomes muscle memory when leaders hold rolling reviews and adjust course without hesitation.
- **Accountability** becomes reflex when teams own outcomes rather than wait for instructions.
- **Communication** becomes instinct when clarity replaces jargon in every meeting.
- **Engagement** becomes second nature when recognition and inclusion are woven into the daily fabric of work.

A framework in memory is fragile. A framework in muscle is unstoppable.

The Shift from Execution to Culture

At first, PACE is about execution. Leaders use it to bridge the gap between vision and results. But over time, something deeper happens: PACE shifts from *what you do* to *who you are.*

Execution becomes culture.
Culture becomes identity.
Identity outlives leadership tenure.

When that shift takes root, even when a leader steps away, the organization continues to execute with clarity, accountability, and engagement. This is how transformation becomes self-sustaining.

Embedding Through Rituals

The bridge between framework and flame is **rituals**. Rituals anchor behaviours until they become second nature.

- **Planning Rituals:** Quarterly rolling reviews where teams reset priorities, not as a bureaucratic exercise but as a moment of clarity.
- **Accountability Rituals:** Ownership dashboards that highlight commitments publicly, making promises visible and progress undeniable.
- **Communication Rituals:** Real-time decision forums where issues are solved in the moment instead of festering in endless threads.
- **Engagement Rituals:** Spontaneous recognition moments – a leader walking the floor, appreciating effort, and igniting pride without scheduling it.

These rituals turn the PACE framework into PACE culture. They create the drumbeat that leaders and teams can march to – steady, consistent, and alive.

When PACE lives in rituals, it can no longer be forgotten. It is no longer "the framework we tried once." It becomes "the way we do things here." That is the moment a framework becomes a flame.

The PACE Leadership Manifesto

Frameworks explain.
Manifestos ignite.

Leaders don't just need tools; they need truths to live by. The following seven principles are not suggestions. They are **unbreakable commitments** that separate leaders who dabble in change from those who embody it. These are the laws of PACE leadership – short, sharp, and unforgettable.

1. Execution is Leadership

Vision is not enough. Strategy is not enough. A leader who cannot move ideas into action is no leader at all. Execution is not a detail beneath leadership – it *is* leadership. Without it, vision is a mirage and strategy is theatre.

2. Clarity Over Complexity

Complexity is the enemy of alignment. When leaders simplify the message, teams move faster, together. Confusion is costly; clarity compounds. The best leaders turn noise into signal, ambiguity into direction, and strategy into simple, actionable steps.

3. Accountability is Freedom

Accountability is not punishment; it is liberation. It frees people from finger-pointing and excuses. When ownership is clear, creativity flourishes. Accountability transforms work from a burden into a choice, from compliance into pride.

4. Communication Creates Culture

Every word is a seed. Some grow into trust; others grow into fear. Leaders must speak with honesty, not spin; clarity, not jargon. Communication is never neutral – it either builds culture or breaks it.

5. Engagement Fuels Energy

People don't follow strategies; they follow passion. Engagement is not about pep talks or posters on the wall. It is about recognition, inclusion, and purpose. When people feel valued, they bring energy. And energy, multiplied across a team, becomes momentum.

6. Consistency Builds Credibility

Anyone can inspire once. But culture is not built on one speech or one town hall. It is built on repetition, rhythm, and constancy. Leaders who show up the same way, day after day, earn trust. Consistency is credibility.

7. Culture is the True Strategy

Strategies change. Markets shift. Technologies disrupt. But culture outlives them all. A strategy may win you a quarter; culture will win you a generation. If culture is strong, strategy finds a way. If culture is weak, strategy collapses on impact.

The Leadership Code

These seven principles are not just reminders; they are a **leadership code**. A code to be recited, embodied, and passed forward.

- When the vision is grand but execution is faltering – return to the code.
- When resistance rises and fatigue spreads – return to the code.
- When technology distracts and uncertainty multiplies – return to the code.

This is the compass of PACE. It does not bend with circumstance. It points leaders back to the flame.

The manifesto is not for the walls of your office. It is for the walls of your heart. Because once it is etched there, every decision you make, every word you speak, every ritual you embed will carry its fire.

Call to Action – Lighting the Flame

Before culture can change, the leader must confront themselves. Ask, with brutal honesty:

- *If I stepped away tomorrow, would my organization continue to execute – or collapse into confusion?*
- *Do my teams act from clarity, or do they wait for permission?*
- *What behaviours have I institutionalized that will outlive my role – and which will vanish with me?*
- *Have I built a culture of accountability and engagement, or a culture of compliance and fear?*

These are not rhetorical questions. They are mirrors. And leadership begins with the courage to look directly into them.

Your 90-Day PACE Commitment

Transformation does not begin with grand gestures. It begins with simple, disciplined steps that light the first flame. Over the next 90 days, choose these three commitments:

- **Within 30 Days:** Establish one ritual of clarity.
  Hold a rolling review, create a dashboard, or simplify a communication channel. One act that makes direction undeniable.
- **Within 60 Days:** Build one accountability loop.
  Make ownership visible. Create a space where commitments are tracked and celebrated, not hidden.
- **Within 90 Days:** Tell one leadership story.
  Share a personal failure, a turnaround moment, or a recognition of your team's grit. Stories carry more weight than strategies. They teach the culture you want to leave behind.

Do not wait for the "perfect plan." Fire does not begin with a bonfire. It begins with a spark.

Think of PACE as fire.

- **The framework is the spark** – it ignites ideas.
- **The rituals are the oxygen** – they sustain behaviours.
- **The culture is the flame** – it spreads, warms, and endures.

A fire left unattended dies. A fire fed with oxygen grows. Leaders are not merely guardians of execution; they are firekeepers of culture. Their task is not to strike sparks once, but to tend the flame so it survives storms, seasons, and successors.

Imagine a relay runner. She runs with full speed, carrying the torch, knowing the finish line is not hers to cross. Her task is simpler and harder – to pass the flame unbroken.

That is leadership. Not to hoard the fire, not to let it flicker, but to ensure it burns brighter in the next hand.

PACE is your torch. Light it in your planning. Feed it with accountability. Protect it with communication. Multiply it through engagement. And when your race is done, pass it forward – not as a framework, but as a flame.

This is the essence of leadership: not frameworks that fade, but flames that endure. May your leadership be the fire that outlives you.